Enquiries of Local Authorities

Fourmat Publishing

Enquiries of Local Authorities
by Keith Pugsley, LL.B, Solicitor,
Director of Law and Administration,
Dacorum Borough Council,
Hemel Hempstead

Second edition

London
Fourmat Publishing
1991

ISBN 1 85190 133 7

First published 1989
Second edition July 1991

All rights reserved

© 1991 KM Pugsley

Published by Fourmat Publishing
133 Upper Street Islington London N1 1QP

Printed in Great Britain by
Billing & Sons Ltd, Worcester

For my wife, Gilly
and my other very good friends

Acknowledgements

Grateful thanks are due to my employers, Dacorum Borough Council, for their encouragement and generous provision of typing and reprographic services. Thanks in particular to Audrey Budd and her enthusiastic team of search assistants who first sparked an interest in the subject and to Maureen Denham and the capable staff of her Central Typing Bureau. Finally I would like to thank Mr. D. Raggatt, Deputy Remembrancer of the City of London, for his invaluable assistance with Local Acts peculiar to the City of London.
KMP
June 1989

Thanks to my wife Gilly for her assistance in the production of this second edition.
KMP
March 1991

Contents   page

Introduction   1
The general notes to Form CON 29   3

PART I Standard Enquiries   7

Enquiry 1:	Development plans provisions	9
Enquiry 2:	Drainage	20
Enquiry 3:	Maintenance of roads etc	27
Enquiry 4:	Road schemes	31
Enquiry 5:	Outstanding notices	35
Enquiry 6:	Building Regulations	40
Enquiry 7:	Planning applications and permissions	43
Enquiry 8:	Notices under Planning Acts	50
Enquiry 9:	Directions restricting permitted development	64
Enquiry 10:	Orders under Planning Acts	67
Enquiry 11:	Compensation for planning decisions	71
Enquiry 12:	Pre-registration conservation area	74
Enquiry 13:	Compulsory purchase	77
Enquiry 14:	Areas designated under Housing Acts etc	79
Enquiry 15:	Smoke control order	85
Enquiry 16:	Contaminated land	89

PART II Optional Enquiries   93

Enquiry 17:	Railways	95
Enquiry 18:	Public paths or byways	99
Enquiry 19:	Permanent road closure	103
Enquiry 20:	Traffic schemes	107
Enquiry 21:	Advertisements	113
Enquiry 22:	Completion notices	122
Enquiry 23:	Parks and countryside	126
Enquiry 24:	Pipe lines	132

Contents

		page
Enquiry 25:	Houses in multiple occupation	136
Enquiry 26:	Noise abatement	139
Enquiry 27:	Urban development areas	143
Enquiry 28:	Enterprise zones	148
Enquiry 29:	Inner urban improvement areas	152
Enquiry 30:	Simplified planning zones	155
Enquiry 31:	Land maintenance notices	159
Enquiry 32:	Mineral consultation areas	162
Enquiry 33:	Hazardous substance consents	165
Appendix:	**Form CON 29**	171
Index		177

Introduction

An integral part of the modern conveyancing process is the conduct of a search of the Register of Local Land Charges maintained by District Councils and the raising of Enquiries of Local Authorities.

The Register of Local Land Charges contains details of all local land charges registered against property situated within the district administered by the Council. The Register contains details of such matters as outstanding liability for road and other financial charges, home improvement grants, tree preservation orders and notices served consequent upon the making of a compulsory purchase order. There are a multitude of local land charges made registrable under Act of Parliament or Regulation; they are outside the scope of this manual.

A purchaser of property, whether freehold or leasehold, will be interested in, and concerned to have, as full a picture as possible of the property he is purchasing. He will want to know, for instance, details of any highways proposals, the position regarding planning permission, and whether the Council has any proposals which will directly or indirectly affect the property he is intending to purchase.

Searches of the Register of Local Land Charges are conducted either in person, by attendance at the offices of the District or London Borough Council, or, much more commonly, by despatch to the District or London Borough Council of Form LLC1, the application for an Official Search of the Register. The purchaser, when lodging his application, will normally send with it Form CON 29 Enquiries of Local Authority. The

ENQUIRIES OF LOCAL AUTHORITIES

form, despatched to the Council in duplicate, contains thirty-three Enquiries designed to reveal to an intending purchaser information about the property to be purchased and the effect on it of the exercise, or proposed exercise, of a wide variety of powers and duties vested in District Councils.

These powers and duties are exercised by the Council's officers on behalf of the Council or one of its committees. The Enquiries about them fall broadly into three categories:

- (i) Technical Services — Enquiries relating to highways, sewers etc.
- (ii) Planning — Enquiries relating to the control of development under the Town and Country Planning Act.
- (iii) Environmental Health — Enquiries relating to control of the physical environment, eg overcrowding, noise abatement, smoke control.

The Enquiries on Form CON 29 are divided into two parts:

Part I Enquiries (Enquiries 1 to 16) will be replied to by the Council for one inclusive fee.

Part II Enquiries (Enquiries 17 to 33) are charged for individually and will only elicit a reply from the Council if the purchaser or his solicitor places a tick in the appropriate box on the front of the form.

It is the purpose of this manual to give a commentary on the Enquiries contained in Form CON 29. Please note that the form is reproduced in the Appendix.

The manual is intended for the guidance of those new to the form and those wanting a ready reference to the meaning of the Enquiries and the implications of the replies given. It is not intended as a comprehensive or definitive interpretation of the law, but rather as a guide and a training tool.

The general notes to Form CON 29

There are seven general notes on Form CON 29. They are of an explanatory nature and are designed for the guidance of users.

Note (A) is a warning to users of the form that the Enquiries and replies given relate to the property as described in Box B of the form. Great care should therefore be taken to ensure that the property is accurately and properly described. For domestic residential properties the full postal address should suffice, but a plan should be attached in the case of open undeveloped sites, or where there is any doubt as to the correct boundary or address of the property. A plan must be attached if Enquiry 18 is raised. This note also warns users that replies given will relate to *any part* of the property enquired about, not merely the entire property. A reply revealing the existence of a proposal for the compulsory purchase of property, for instance, may relate to only a tiny portion of the property enquired about. Any purchaser in doubt should make further enquiries independently of Form CON 29. Finally, this note makes it clear to users that any reference to "the area" (see, for example, Enquiries 12, 14, 15, 26 and 27) means an area in which the property enquired about is situated.

Note (B) is a warning to users of the form that: (i) the Enquiries will not reveal information other than that relating to the property specified by the enquirer, so that care should be taken, as mentioned above, to identify correctly and accurately the property enquired about. Further enquiries of adjoining properties should be made on a separate Form CON

29 or by a visit to the Council's offices; (ii) matters relating to land outside the administrative area of the Council concerned will not necessarily be revealed. If the property enquired about crosses local government administrative boundaries, the prudent purchaser should enquire of both, or all, Councils concerned; (iii) matters outside the functions of the Council to which the form is sent will not necessarily be revealed. For instance, in non-metropolitan districts, the County Council is the highway authority, and the District Council to which the Form CON 29 is despatched may not be competent to reply fully to highways Enquiries. However, as the note points out, there are frequently agency and other arrangements in existence between County and District Councils whereby Enquiries addressed to the District Council will elicit information from both Councils. If in doubt, the prudent purchaser should enquire of the District Council whether the replies given are comprehensive or whether a further approach should be made to the relevant County Council.

Note (C) makes it clear that references in the Enquiries to "the Council" are intended to include references to any officer or committee or sub-committee exercising the powers on its behalf and to any Council which has exercised those powers in the past but been superseded by the present Council as a result of local government reorganisation in 1974.

Note (D) makes it clear that any references to Acts of Parliament or orders (and there are many of these in the Enquiries) include references to both earlier legislation replaced by current legislation and subsequent modifications or re-enactment of current legislation. This obviates the necessity for frequent revision of Form CON 29. For example, references in the Enquiries to the Town and Country Planning Act 1990 will include references to the Town and Country Planning Act 1962. References to several of the enactments and regulations in the current edition of CON 29 will, in view of current rapid change in Town and Country Planning and Environmental Protection legislation, soon be replaced. By virtue of this note, this replacement does not affect the validity of the Enquiry or the replies given.

Note (E) merely mentions the abbreviation in the Enquiries, of Town and Country Planning Act, Order or Regulation to T&CP Act 1990 etc. This abbreviation is used in Part I Enquiries 1 and 11 and Part II Enquiries 22, 30, 31 and 32.

The general notes to Form CON 29

Note (F) is a warning that Councils or their officers will only be legally liable for the replies given to the Enquiries in the event of negligence. It is essential that a Council's registers and records are kept up to date on a daily basis since negligent replies may result in claims for substantial damages against the Council giving them. Although these claims will normally be met by the Council's insurers, a proliferation of such claims may result in either a substantial increase in the Council's insurance premium or even a refusal by the insurance company to renew a policy. It may not be a defence to such a claim to show that the officer replying to a particular Enquiry had not been advised by another officer of the necessity to amend or update the records. Liability extends to any purchaser of the property who had knowledge of the replies to Enquiries before entering into a contract for the purchase, whether or not the Enquiries were raised on his behalf.

Note (G) explains the status of the Enquiries. The form is approved by The Law Society (the professional body representing the interests of solicitors who, in practice, raise the Enquiries on behalf of their clients) and the various associations representing the interests of the Councils replying to the Enquiries. It is published by their authority so that it can be assumed that the Enquiries have been carefully designed to elicit information relevant to the property and which the purchaser will generally be concerned to have, and that the Councils have agreed to reply to the Enquiries on receipt of their reasonable charges. Additional specific enquiries may of course also be raised and these will be separately charged for.

Part I Standard Enquiries

All of these Enquiries will be replied to by the Council, unless there is insufficient information in the search application or the Council's records to enable a reply to be made. The composite fee remitted by the purchaser or his solicitor will cover all these Enquiries.

Enquiry 1: Development plans provisions

Structure Plan
1.1.1. What structure plan is in force?
1.1.2. Have any proposals been made public for the alteration of the structure plan?

Local Plans
1.2. What local plans (including action area plans) are adopted or in the course of preparation?

Old Style Development Plan
1.3. What old style development plan is in force?

Unitary Plan
1.4.1. What stage has been reached in the preparation of a unitary development plan?
1.4.2. Have any proposals been made public for the alteration or replacement of a unitary development plan?

Non-Statutory Plan
1.5.1. Have the Council made public any proposals for the preparation or modification of a non-statutory plan?
1.5.2. If so, what stage has been reached?

Primary Use and Provisions for the Property
1.6. In any of the above plans or proposals:
   (a) what primary use is indicated for the area?
   (b) what provisions are included for the property?

CON 29: PART I STANDARD ENQUIRIES

Land required for Public Purposes
1.7. Is the property included in any of the categories of land specified in Schedule 13 paras 5 and 6 of the T&CP Act 1990?

This Enquiry concerns statutory structure and local plans prepared and adopted by local planning authorities under the Town and Country Planning Act and non-statutory plans.

Structure plans are the responsibility of the County Councils, and set the planning scene county-wide. They are broad general statements of principles relating to housing policies, shopping policies, transport, industry, commerce, the Green Belt, etc and cover a wide variety of economic, ecological, environmental and other issues. Under the Town and Country Planning Act, all County Councils must carry out a survey of their area to examine all those matters which may affect the development of the county from a town planning point of view. Those matters which must be examined and kept under review by the County Councils include, for example:

(i) The physical and economic characteristics of the area, including the main purposes for which land is used, eg agricultural, industrial, commercial, residential, etc.
(ii) Population size, distribution and constitution.
(iii) Communications, transport and traffic.
(iv) Projected changes in any of the above.

Having conducted the survey, the County Council must then prepare and send to the Secretary of State for approval a structure plan covering the above matters. The structure plan is more than just a map. In fact it is principally a written document detailing the county policies and proposals in respect of development and land use within the area of the plan, including proposals for improvement of the environment. It will be illustrated by diagrams and maps and be accompanied by an "explanatory memorandum" summarising and explaining the policies.

Once formulated, the structure plan will be submitted to the Secretary of State for the Environment for approval, but must first be advertised, placed on deposit at the Council's offices for public inspection and an opportunity given for objections to be made to it by the public or interested bodies.

The Secretary of State then considers the plan and may reject

Enquiry 1: Development plans provisions

it, approve it or modify it. If he decides to approve it, he will first cause there to be an "examination in public" which is in effect a public inquiry at which objectors will be able to state their case and the County Council will attempt to answer the objections.

Eventually the structure plan will be approved by the Secretary of State with or without modifications.

In relation to Greater London, the structure plan is called the Greater London Development Plan and this structure plan continues in force notwithstanding the abolition of the Greater London Council until such time as a unitary development plan for a particular borough becomes operative. Once such a unitary development plan is approved by the Secretary of State, he may by order revoke that part of the Greater London Development Plan as is covered by the new unitary development plan or that part of it which has come into force.

Summary

Enquiry 1.1.1 asks for the name of the structure plan to be stated. If a structure plan has not yet been finalised, the purchaser may be concerned to know what stage has been reached in the preparation of a structure plan for the area including the property. The purchaser will expect to be told whether a draft has been submitted to the Secretary of State for approval, whether it has reached examination in public, etc, or whether it has actually been approved.

* * *

At any time after the structure plan has come into operation, the County Council may submit proposals to the Secretary of State for its alteration, and all such proposals must go through a similar procedure as the original structure plan, except that sometimes the examination in public may be dispensed with.

Summary

Enquiry 1.1.2 asks whether there are any known proposals for alteration of the structure plan which have been made public. A purchaser will be interested to know if there are since, for

CON 29: PART I STANDARD ENQUIRIES

example, he may be buying a property in an area which is shortly to be designated for industrial development.

* * *

As structure plans are the responsibility of the County Councils and set out broad trends of policy, so **local plans** are the responsibility of District Councils and have more specific and detailed provisions. It is from the local plan, rather than the structure plan, that a purchaser will learn what effect the local Council's planning proposals will have on the property he is buying. Action area plans may also be prepared by the District Council. These are local plans prepared for part of the area of the local authority which has been selected for comprehensive treatment by development, redevelopment or improvement.

The local plan is prepared generally in conformity with the broad principles of the structure plan but it is prepared by the District Council and, in preparing it, the District Council may take into account the survey conducted by the County Council in connection with the structure plan.

The local plan will consist of a map and a written statement and may be accompanied by diagrams and other descriptive matter. It will include policies for housing, employment, industry, shopping, the Green Belt and other details of permitted land use and development within the District Council's area.

Similar to the structure plan, a local plan when drafted must be publicised and opportunity given for representations by the public. The local plan need not normally be submitted to the Secretary of State for approval in the same way as a structure plan, but the District Council must normally hold a public local inquiry into objections before formally adopting the local plan by resolution of the Council.

The District Council may from time to time make proposals for altering or replacing a local plan, and the procedure is similar to that for the preparation of a local plan.

Summary

Enquiry 1.2 asks for a statement of the local plans (including any action area plans) which have been adopted or are in the

Enquiry 1: Development plans provisions

course of preparation. A purchaser will be concerned to know what stage has been reached in the preparation of a local plan for the area including the property. A purchaser will expect to be told whether a draft has been prepared, whether it has been published, whether public representations have been invited, an inquiry held or whether the local plan has been adopted.

There may be published proposals for the alteration of an adopted local plan. A purchaser will be interested to know if there are since there may, for example, be a proposal to designate the area in which he is buying his house as prime for industrial development.

* * *

The procedure for the preparation and adoption of structure plans and local plans was introduced by the Town and Country Planning Act 1971. Previously the requirement was for the County Council to carry out its survey and produce what is now called an "old style development plan". Some of these plans still survive.

A **development plan** under the old style procedure indicated both the manner in which the land covered by the plan was to be used and the stages by which that development was to be carried out. Development plans consist of a basic map, written statement and other illustrative maps or plans, including sometimes town maps indicating particular proposals for a town, comprehensive development area maps indicating proposals for complete redevelopment of particular areas and a programme map showing the stages by which the proposals contained in the written statement should be carried out.

Development plans may allocate specific areas for agricultural, residential, industrial or other purposes, define sites for proposed roads, buildings, airfields, parks, nature reserves and pleasure gardens and define areas of comprehensive development.

Summary

Enquiry 1.3 asks whether one of these old style development plans affects the property. If one of these plans is revealed, the purchaser will want to know whether the primary use of the area including the property is indicated, or whether any specific provisions are proposed for the property. A purchaser will want to know full details of any such proposals so that he will be sure of what use he may be permitted to make of the property.

* * *

London and the metropolitan authorities

On 1 April 1986 the Greater London Council was abolished by the Local Government Act 1985, and the London Borough Councils became the local planning authorities for their respective boroughs. Schedule 1 of the Local Government Act 1985 applied to the local planning authorities (London Borough Councils) for the purposes of preparation of development plans instead of Part II of the Town and Country Planning Act 1971 which applied to local planning authorities in the rest of the country. The Town and Country Planning Act 1990 now provides for the system of unitary development plans, introduced by the Local Government Act 1985, and applicable to development plans within Greater London and the metropolitan authorities.

The provisions of the Town and Country Planning Act relating to the system of unitary development plans apply to a local planning authority with effect from such date as may be appointed in relation to the area in question by an order of the Secretary of State.

Once the Secretary of State has made an order bringing the Act into effect within a particular London borough or metropolitan area, the Council, as local planning authority, will have a duty to keep under review matters affecting the planning and development of the area, and may institute surveys of the area for this purpose. The matters for survey and review by the Council will include:
  (i) physical and economic characteristics of the area including principal land uses;
 (ii) size, composition and distribution of population;
(iii) communications, transport and traffic;
(iv) projected changes in any of the above.

Within a time to be prescribed by the Secretary of State, the Council must prepare for its area a "unitary development plan".

Enquiry 1: Development plans provisions

Unitary development plans are to be comprised of two parts:

Part I a written statement formulating the Council's general development and land use policies for the area (including traffic management and environmental improvement provisions).

Part II detailed proposals for development or land use in the area;

a map showing the proposals on a geographical basis;

a reasoned justification of the policies and proposals, diagrams, illustrations and descriptive or explanatory matter.

The proposals in Part II must be in general conformity with the general policy in Part I.

In preparing the unitary development plan as outlined above and before finally determining its contents, the Council must secure that publicity is given to the proposals and that the public and interested bodies have an opportunity to make representations on them. Any representations made must be considered by the Council. Once the plan is prepared, before it is adopted by the Council as local planning authority, copies must be made available for inspection at its offices and a time given in which objections may be made.

A copy of the unitary development plan as published must be sent to the Secretary of State, together with a statement of the steps taken to publicise it and of the consultations which have taken place and the views of interested parties. The Secretary of State may require the Council to conduct further consultation.

After the period for objections has expired and any objections have been considered by the Council, the Council may adopt the plan by resolution either as originally prepared or as modified to take account of objections and representations. The plan becomes operational on the date of this resolution.

The Council, as local planning authority, may hold a local inquiry to hear and debate objections made to the proposals contained in the unitary development plan before it is adopted. The inquiry will be presided over by the Secretary of State or, in certain circumstances, by a person appointed by the Council.

At any time before it is formally adopted by the Council the Secretary of State may "call it in" for his approval, and if he does the Council may take no further steps in its adoption until the Secretary of State has reached a decision. He may, in the event, approve of the plan with or without modification, or reject it, giving reasons. If it is approved, the Council may then adopt it, having made any appropriate modifications as directed by the Secretary of State. The Secretary of State may decide to call a public local inquiry into objections before approving the plan for adoption by the Council. If the provisions of the Town and Country Planning Act relating to unitary development plans have not been brought into force within the borough, existing local plans and any old development plans in existence will still be relevant in a consideration of the uses and developments for which planning permission will be granted.

Summary

Enquiry 1.4.1 asks what stage has been reached in the preparation of a unitary development plan. The purchaser will want to know whether a draft plan has been prepared, whether it has reached the publicity stage, whether objections have been invited, whether the plan has been submitted to the Secretary of State as a "call in", or adopted, or whether a public local inquiry is to be held into objections. This part of the Enquiry is relevant only within London boroughs and metropolitan areas.

* * *

Unitary development plans may be subject to alteration from time to time either on proposals made by the Council as local planning authority or by the Secretary of State. Any alterations to a plan which has been approved by the Secretary of State other than certain minor alterations (for which there is an alternative shorter procedure) must go through the complete publicity, objection, inquiry and adoption procedure outlined above.

Summary

Enquiry 1.4.2 asks whether there are any proposals for the alteration or replacement of such a plan. A purchaser will

Enquiry 1: Development plans provisions

want to know if there are any such proposals, what they amount to and what stage in the publicity/consultation objection or approval stage they have reached, and how they affect the property he is proposing to purchase. This part of the Enquiry will only generally reveal what proposals have been made and the stage they have reached. An affirmative response will provoke a prudent purchaser to enquire after further details or to inspect the proposals personally in order to discover the effect they may have, if approved and adopted, on the property concerned.

* * *

Structure plans, local plans, unitary plans and old style development plans are all "statutory plans" since the requirement to prepare them is imposed on Councils by statute, namely the Town and Country Planning Act. Councils responsible for town planning may however make, of their own decision, "non-statutory plans", that is plans covering particular areas or particular issues. For instance, town plans may be prepared covering detailed proposals for development within particular towns. The public will be invited to participate in the plan-making process and interested bodies will be asked for their comments. Eventually, after having passed through a similar process to that involved in the preparation of statutory plans (but without submission to the Secretary of State) the Council will adopt the final plan as planning policy for the area it covers. Such plans do not have the same status as statutory plans but may be relied upon at public local inquiries into refusals of planning permission since they will have gone through a public consultation process and have been finally adopted by a body of elected councillors.

Summary

Enquiry 1.5.1 asks whether the Council has published any proposals to prepare or alter a non-statutory plan which affects the property. A purchaser will be interested in the details of any such proposals.

Enquiry 1.5.2 asks what stage any such non-statutory plan has reached, ie has it been proposed, published, objections invited or whether it has been formally approved.

CON 29: PART I STANDARD ENQUIRIES

* * *

The written statement or the proposals map which forms part of the local plan will indicate by different notations the primary uses to which certain areas are to be put, and may exceptionally make particular reference to individual properties or groups of properties. For example, the plan may identify prime industrial or shopping areas, land earmarked for public open space, agricultural priority areas or areas of archaeological importance. These notations will mean that preference will be given to developments of the kind conforming to those notations in the areas which they cover.

A unitary development plan will indicate by reference to its written statement and proposals map (on a geographical basis) primary uses to which particular areas of land should be put, and for which there will be a presumption in favour of granting planning permission. It may also indicate specific proposals for particular property within the area. Part II of the plan may designate any part of the area to which it relates as an "action area", ie an area selected for comprehensive treatment by development, redevelopment or improvement, and in these action areas the plan will contain a detailed description of the proposed treatment of the area.

Non-statutory plans may also identify primary uses and particular proposals for properties within the area.

Summary

Enquiry 1.6.(a) asks, in relation to any structure, local, old style, unitary or non-statutory plans, what primary use is indicated for the area. The answer is important to the purchaser as it might affect the use to which he wishes to put the property he is proposing to purchase, and the availability or otherwise of planning permission for that use.

Enquiry 1.6.(b) asks for details of any specific provisions included within the plans for the property. The reply to this part of this Enquiry may be decisive as to whether the purchaser decides to proceed with the purchase.

* * *

The Town and Country Planning Act provides that where land is affected by provisions of statutory structure and local

Enquiry 1: Development plans provisions

plans which provide for it to be protected from development in the interests of the future needs of the Government or Council or a statutory undertaker (gas, water, electricity, etc) so that its value for sale is affected, an owner may serve a "blight notice" on the Council requiring the Council to purchase the whole of the land concerned. If, for instance, land is so protected from development by the plans as it will be required at some time in the future for highway improvement, this will obviously affect its value since a purchaser will be deterred from buying it.

Paragraphs 5 and 6 of Schedule 13 to the Town and Country Planning Act extend these provisions to include any proposals contained in non-statutory plans.

Summary

Enquiry 1.7 asks whether the property or any part of it is affected by provisions of a non-statutory plan which effectively prohibit development in the interests of preserving the Council's plans for the future. A purchaser will require a negative response, and an affirmative response will almost certainly deter the purchaser from proceeding to buy the property.

Enquiry 2: Drainage

Foul Drainage
2.1.1. To the Council's knowledge, does foul drainage from the property drain to a public sewer?
2.1.2. If so, is the connection to the public sewer effected by:
 (a) drain and private sewer, or
 (b) drain alone?

Surface Water Drainage
2.2.1. Does surface water from the property drain to a public sewer?
2.2.2. Does surface water from the property drain to a highway drain or sewer which is the subject of an agreement under s.21(1)(a) of the Public Health Act 1936?
2.2.3. If the Reply to either 2.2.1 or 2.2.2 is "Yes", is the connection to that sewer or highway drain effected by:
 (a) drain and private sewer, or
 (b) drain alone?

Combined Private Sewer
2.3. Is there in force in relation to any part of the drainage of the property an agreement under s.22 of the Building Act 1984?

Adoption Agreement
2.4.1. To the Council's knowledge, is any sewer serving, or which is proposed to serve, the property the

Enquiry 2: Drainage

> *subject of an agreement under s.18 of the Public Health Act 1936?*
> 2.4.2. *If so, is such an agreement supported by a bond or other financial security?*
>
> **Potential Compulsory Drainage Connection**
> 2.5. *If the Reply to either Enquiry 2.1.1 or 2.2.1 is "No", to the Council's knowledge, is there a foul or surface water sewer (as appropriate) within 100 feet of the property and at a level which makes it reasonably practicable to construct a drain from the property to that sewer?*
>
> **Sewerage Undertaker**
> 2.6. *Please state the name and address of the sewerage undertaker.*

This Enquiry relates to the drainage and sewerage of the property and responsibility for maintenance of drains and sewers.

A **drain** generally conveys effluent from one building or a group of buildings within one curtilage and deposits it in a sewer, cesspool or septic tank. Responsibility for maintenance of a drain is that of the property owner and the drain remains in private ownership.

A **sewer** conveys the effluent to a sewage treatment works. It generally runs under a road but may be in public or private ownership. It serves more than one property.

Foul drainage is effluent produced from within the premises.

Surface water drainage consists of rain water.

Summary

Enquiry 2.1.1 asks whether *foul drainage* from the premises drains into a public sewer, ie a sewer owned and maintained by the water authorities, rather than into a cesspool or septic tank. A purchaser will prefer a positive reply since drainage into a cesspool or septic tank will involve the owner in maintenance costs in respect of the latter and will require occasional emptying at further cost, whereas drainage into a public sewer ensures the effluent is eventually treated at a treatment works. As the footnote to this part of the Enquiry

21

mentions, the reply given will be based on information supplied to the Council by the sewerage undertakers. The Council may be the agent for the sewerage undertaker.

* * *

If there is a public sewer, drainage into it from the premises may be direct by drain, or, if the premises are at some distance from the public sewer, there may be an intervening private sewer, the responsibility for maintenance of which will belong either to the owner of the premises, or be shared between him and a number of other such owners.

Summary

Enquiry 2.1.2 asks whether the connection between the premises and the public sewer is effected by drain alone, or by drain and private sewer. A purchaser will normally prefer a positive response to 2.1.2.(b) and a negative response to 2.1.2.(a) since his maintenance responsibilities will be less for a drain than for a private sewer.

* * *

Surface water, ie rainwater, lands on the roof of the premises and generally runs down the roof and into a series of gutters. From there it will pass along the gutters and into downpipes and then eventually underground. Surface water may drain straight into the ground into what is known as a "soakaway", but more commonly it will flow into a drain and thence into a sewer, and often it will be the same sewer as that which takes the foul drainage.

Summary

Enquiry 2.2.1 asks whether the surface water drainage is to a public sewer, ie a sewer maintainable by the water authority. A purchaser will prefer an affirmative answer.

* * *

Drains or sewers may belong to the County Council (or London Borough or Metropolitan Council) in its capacity as highway authority if the drains or sewers run in or under the

Enquiry 2: Drainage

highway. Water authorities may enter into agreements with these Councils under s 21(1) (a) of the Public Health Act 1936 enabling the water authority to use these drains or sewers for the purposes of draining surface water from premises or streets.

Summary

Enquiry 2.2.2 asks whether surface water from the premises drains to a sewer or highway drain which is subject to one of these agreements.

* * *

Where the reply to either 2.2.1 or 2.2.2 is in the affirmative the purchaser will want to know, if possible, whether the connection to the sewer or highway drain is effected directly by drain or by way of drain and private sewer.

Summary

Enquiry 2.2.3 asks whether the connection between the premises and the sewer or highway drain is effected directly or indirectly.

* * *

Section 22 of the Building Act 1984 makes provision for the combined drainage of buildings. The section provides that, when the drains of buildings are first being laid, if it appears to the authority that those buildings may be drained more economically or advantageously in combination into an existing sewer by means of a private sewer, the authority may require this to be done, either by those constructing the buildings or by the authority on their behalf. The authority will then determine the proportions of the expense of constructing and maintaining the private sewer to be borne by the owners or, in any case where the distance of the existing sewer from the site of any of the buildings in question is more than 100 feet, the authority may agree to accept responsibility for part of the cost.

CON 29: PART I STANDARD ENQUIRIES

Summary

Enquiry 2.3 asks whether there is such an agreement in force under s 22 of the Building Act (formerly s 38 of the Public Health Act) which affects the premises. A purchaser will normally prefer a negative reply since he will generally prefer his premises to drain direct to a public sewer. Maintenance of private sewers, even if shared, can be an expensive business and there will often be arguments between landowners as to when a private sewer requires maintenance.

* * *

Developers constructing new buildings may enter into agreements with the authority whereby the developer will construct the sewer or sewage disposal works necessary to serve the development and, subject to the works being satisfactorily completed to a sufficient standard, the authority will declare the sewer vested in itself and assume responsibility for future maintenance. Such agreements are entered into under s 18 of the Public Health Act 1936 and are commonly referred to as s 18 agreements. They are very often associated with agreements under s 38 of the Highways Act 1980 in respect of new roads.

Summary

Enquiry 2.4.1 asks whether any sewer existing or proposed to serve the premises is subject to a s 18 agreement. Normally a purchaser of a newly constructed house will expect such an agreement to be in force. Therefore he will expect an affirmative response. As the footnote to this part of this Enquiry points out, the enquirer should make similar enquiries of the sewerage undertaker, particularly in respect of newly constructed properties. The Council to which Form CON 29 is sent may act as agent for the sewerage undertaker.

* * *

If such an agreement is in force, the agreement should be supported by a bond, much as a s 38 (Highways Act) agreement should be. The bond is a financial commitment on the part of a financial institution such as a bank, insurance company or pension fund, guaranteeing due performance of the agreement. It will be for the purchaser to satisfy himself that the bond is of a sufficient size to ensure completion of the works on the sewer so that it will be adopted by the authority, and this point is reinforced by the footnote to this part of the Enquiry.

Summary

Enquiry 2.4.2 asks whether there is a bond to support any agreement entered into under s 18 of the Public Health Act. The purchaser will expect an affirmative response if the reply to 2.4.1 was affirmative. If there is no such bond, the purchaser will have to worry about the prospects of his property being drained into a public sewer or the expense he may be put to in ensuring a connection, if the developer goes bankrupt.

* * *

If either foul or surface water drainage is not to a public sewer, the purchaser will want to know whether a foul or surface water sewer is available within a reasonable distance so that a connection can be made. Section 34 of the Public Health Act confers the right on the owner or occupier of premises to have his drains or sewer connected to the public sewer and to discharge both foul and surface water into it. The right is generally limited to the discharge of "domestic sewage" or surface or storm water, and is exercisable on service of 21 days' notice on the water authority who may refuse to permit the connection if, for example, the condition of the drain or sewer to be connected is such that the making of the connection would be prejudicial to the sewerage system.

Summary

Enquiry 2.5 asks whether the Council is aware of the existence of a foul or surface water sewer within 100 feet of the property to which a connection could be made. If there is no public sewer connection, the purchaser will be looking for an affirmative answer here, but the Council may have insufficient information to enable it to reply, in which case the purchaser is instructed, by the footnote to this part of the Enquiry, to make his own survey.

CON 29: PART I STANDARD ENQUIRIES

* * *

The Water Act 1989 provided for the privatisation of the water industry in England and Wales. From 1 September 1989, water and sewerage functions formerly performed by the water authorities were transferred to the new public limited companies by virtue of s 4 of the Act. It is now the duty of the newly formed sewerage undertakers to provide, improve and extend the system of public sewers and to cleanse and maintain them. By virtue of s 73 of the Act, local authorities may enter into agency arrangements with the new undertakers to carry out sewerage functions on their behalf, and this they may do singly or by way of consortium arrangements with other local authorities.

Summary

Enquiry 2.6 asks for the name and address of the relevant sewerage undertaker. A purchaser will need this information, particularly if the Council to which Form CON 29 has been sent has not entered into agency arrangements with the undertaker, since all relevant proposals and decisions on the public sewerage system will be made by the sewerage undertaker.

Enquiry 3: Maintenance of roads etc

Publicly Maintained
3.1. Are all the roadways, footpaths and footways referred to in Boxes B and C on page 1 maintainable at the public expense within the meaning of the Highways Act 1980?

Resolutions to make up or adopt
3.2. If not, have the Council passed any resolution to:
   (a) make up any of those roadways, footpaths or footways at the cost of the frontagers, or
   (b) adopt any of them without cost to the frontagers?
   If so, please specify.

Adoption Agreements
3.3.1. Have the Council entered into any outstanding agreement relating to the adoption of any of those roadways, footpaths or footways? If so, please specify.
3.3.2. Is any such agreement supported by a bond or other financial security?

This Enquiry deals with the respective liabilities of (a) the property owner and (b) the Council for maintenance of highways.

The principal piece of legislation concerned with the classification, creation, maintenance and improvement of highways is the Highways Act 1980.

CON 29: PART I STANDARD ENQUIRIES

A **roadway** is not defined in the Act but may be taken to be that portion of the highway over which vehicles travel, defined in the Act as the "carriageway".

A **footpath** is defined as "a highway over which the public have a right of way on foot only, not being a footway".

A **footway** is defined as "a way comprised in a highway which also comprises a carriageway, being a way over which the public have a right of way on foot only".

Thus a highway, for the purposes of this Enquiry, will normally consist either of a roadway, with or without footway, or of a public footpath. Footpaths, as such, are more often than not unmade and they often cross or border on open fields. Footways on the other hand can only exist in conjunction with a "carriageway" or "roadway" to use the wording of this Enquiry.

Highways, as defined above, are either maintainable at the public expense, or not so maintainable.

Maintainable highways (generally called "adopted highways") are the responsibility of the highway authority, and it is the highway authority for the particular highway which bears the cost of maintenance and repair.

Highways which are not maintainable at the public expense (so-called "unadopted roads") are still highways and may be used by the public as carriageways or footpaths (or bridleways). Maintenance of their surface, however, is the responsibility of the owner of the land over which they run.

Summary

Enquiry 3.1 seeks information as to the responsibility for maintenance of highways described in the Description of the Property appearing on the front of CON 29 and the purchaser will hope for an affirmative reply. If the reply is in the negative, he will know that he may be required to contribute towards the costs of highway maintenance which could be considerable. When completing CON 29, the enquirer should take particular care to ensure that all roads or parts of roads abutting on or leading to the property are accurately described in Boxes B and C on the form.

* * *

Enquiry 3: Maintenance of roads etc

The Highways Act contains a Private Street Works Code which provides for the making-up of private streets by the highway authority. Where the highway authority has inspected a private street and it is not, to its satisfaction, "sewered levelled paved metalled flagged channelled made good and lighted", the authority may decide to carry out street works and recover the cost of those works from the owners of premises fronting the street.

Summary

Enquiry 3.2.(a) enquires whether the Council has decided to use its powers under the Code to make up private roads, footpaths or footways at the cost of the frontagers. The purchaser of the property will hope for a negative reply but if an affirmative reply is given, he will want to know the likely cost of the proposed works and what proportion of them he will be expected to bear.

* * *

Where street works have been carried out in a private street, the Council, if it is satisfied with those works, may adopt the private street as a highway maintainable at the public expense, and take over responsibility for its maintenance. This it may do simply by posting a notice in a prominent position in the highway, declaring the highway to be maintainable at public expense, unless the majority of the owners of the highway object to it being adopted within one month.

Summary

Enquiry 3.2.(b) enquires whether the Council has agreed to adopt a private street when the works have been done, at no further cost to the frontagers. If the purchaser has discovered that the property he wishes to purchase lies in a private street, he will be delighted to find that it is to be made up and adopted at no cost to himself; he will therefore be looking for an affirmative reply to this part of the question if the reply to Enquiry 3.1 was in the negative.

* * *

Under s 38 of the Highways Act, a developer who wishes to construct a new road or roads to service a new development (generally residential) may enter into an agreement with the Council whereby the developer agrees to make up the roads, footways, etc, and to provide drainage and lighting, to adoption standard. The Council, in the same agreement, agrees to adopt the roads and footways as highways maintainable at the public expense. In this way the developer divests himself of future responsibility for maintenance. These agreements are commonly called s 38 agreements.

Summary

Enquiry 3.3.1 enquires whether such an agreement has been entered into. An affirmative reply will indicate to the purchaser that the road will, subject to its being made up to adoption standard by the developer, be adopted, and he will have no future responsibility for its maintenance. The purchaser will be looking for an affirmative reply if the reply to Enquiry 3.1 was in the negative.

* * *

If a s 38 agreement has been entered into by a developer, it will normally be supported by a bond. A bond is a financial commitment entered into by a financial institution such as a bank, insurance company, etc whereby the financial institution agrees to pay to the Council a specified sum of money in the event that the developer fails for whatever reason to make the road up to adoption standard. The sum of money should be sufficient to pay for any outstanding works necessary to bring the road up to adoption standard. As works proceed on the road, the bond sum will probably be reduced, with the consent of the Council, to such sum as will still be adequate to carry out the outstanding works.

Summary

Enquiry 3.3.2 enquires whether there is a bond in existence supporting the s 38 agreement referred to in any reply to Enquiry 3.3.1. If the reply is in the affirmative, the purchaser will have to satisfy himself by inquiry and inspection as to the adequacy of the amount of the bond to secure completion of any outstanding road works under the agreement. If there is a s 38 agreement but no bond, the purchaser will be put on notice that there is a possibility that the road will not be adopted or at least not without expense to himself.

Enquiry 4: Road schemes

Trunk and Special Roads

4.1.1. What orders, draft orders or schemes have been notified to the Council by the appropriate Secretary of State for the construction of a new trunk or special road, the centre line of which is within 200 metres of the property?

4.1.2. What proposals have been notified to the Council by the appropriate Secretary of State for the alteration or improvement of an existing road, involving the construction, whether or not within existing highway limits, of a subway, underpass, flyover, footbridge, elevated road or dual carriageway, the centre line of which is within 200 metres of the property?

Other Roads

4.2. What proposals of their own have the Council approved for any of the following, the limits of construction of which are within 200 metres of the property:
   (a) the construction of a new road, or
   (b) the alteration or improvement of an existing road, involving the construction, whether or not within existing highway limits, of a subway, underpass, flyover, footbridge, elevated road or dual carriageway?

Road Proposals Involving Acquisition

4.3. What proposals have the Council approved, or

CON 29: PART I STANDARD ENQUIRIES

> have been notified to the Council by the appropriate Secretary of State, for highway construction or improvement that involve the acquisition of the property?
>
> **Road Proposals at Consultation Stage**
> 4.4. What proposals have either the Secretary of State or the Council published for public consultation relating to the construction of a new road indicating a possible route the centre line of which would be likely to be within 200 metres of the property?

This Enquiry deals with proposals to construct new roads which may affect the property in the future.

Special roads are roads reserved for particular classes of traffic.

Trunk roads are major roads which generally stretch over considerable distances through several districts and counties. They are the responsibility of the Secretary of State for Transport, ie central government. Before constructing a new trunk road, the Secretary of State must make an order defining the route of the proposed new road. If there are any objections to the proposals, these must generally be subjected to examination at a public local inquiry before the order can be confirmed. The Secretary of State is obliged to notify the Council in advance of his proposals for new roads. If the proposal is to construct a new road the centre line of which will be within 200 metres of the property to be purchased, the purchaser will want to know full details of the proposals.

Summary

Enquiry 4.1.1 enquires whether there are any published proposals for a new road the centre line of which, if the proposal is adopted, would be within 200 metres of any part of the property. Ideally the purchaser will be looking for a negative reply to this part of the question since, although he may qualify for compensation from the Department of Transport should the proposal be adopted, the existence of a new trunk road less than 200 metres away from a property will often deter a future purchaser.

Enquiry 4: Road schemes

Enquiry 4.1.2 makes a similar enquiry regarding proposals for the alteration or improvement of existing roads, where such improvements etc involve the construction of a subway, underpass, flyover, footbridge, elevated road or dual carriageway. Again, the 200 metres is to be taken from the centre line to the nearest part of the property affected.

* * *

New roads other than trunk roads may be constructed by the Council itself, generally as part of a development scheme involving a new housing project.

Summary

Enquiry 4.2.(a) asks whether the Council has approved any proposals for the construction of new roads the centre line of which would lie within 200 metres of any part of the property searched against. The footnote to this part of the Enquiry makes it clear that it relates only to the Council's own proposals, not to those of other bodies or companies.

Enquiry 4.2.(b) makes a similar enquiry regarding proposals for the alteration or improvement of existing roads, involving the construction of a subway, underpass, flyover, footbridge, elevated road or dual carriageway. Again, the 200 metres is to be taken from the centre line of the proposed improvement to the nearest part of the property affected. As with Enquiry 4.2.(a) this part of the Enquiry relates only to proposals of the Council, not to those of other bodies or companies, which the Council, wearing its local planning authority hat, may be asked to approve.

* * *

If there are proposals, either by the Secretary of State or the Council, for the construction of a new road or improvement of an existing road, these will often involve the acquisition of land by the Secretary of State or the Council, as appropriate, to enable the scheme to proceed. The Secretary of State or the Council may be able to acquire the land by agreement, but failing this the use of compulsory purchase powers will be necessary. Under ss 239–246 Highways Act, both the Secretary of State and the Council acting as highway authority have extensive powers of compulsory acquisition of land for highway construction and improvement.

Summary

Enquiry 4.3 asks whether any road proposals approved by the Council or notified to the Council by the Secretary of State will involve the acquisition of the property or any part of it. The purchaser here will again prefer a negative reply, for although compensation will be due to him for the loss of his land, the precise amount of land to be lost, or the compensation to be paid for it, will be unclear for a considerable time.

* * *

Before the preparation and formal submission for confirmation of orders made by the Secretary of State or the Council for new road schemes, there will be a lengthy period of consultation with interested parties and the public. Full details of proposals will be published for inspection by the public, and the public will be invited to comment on them. This will take place at an early stage in the process, the intention being to test public reaction to the proposals before the formal orders are adopted.

Summary

Enquiry 4.4. asks whether this preliminary consultation stage has been reached in connection with any road proposals which indicate a possible route of the proposed new road lying within 200 metres of the property enquired about. In this case the proposal will be indicated by a line or series of lines on a map and if any part of the property lies within 200 metres of that line this question will be answered in the affirmative.

Enquiry 5: Outstanding notices

What outstanding statutory notices or informal notices have been issued by the Council under the Public Health Acts, Housing Acts or Highways Acts? (This enquiry does not cover notices shown in the Official Certificate of Search or notices relating to matters covered by Enquiry 13.)

This Enquiry relates to notices in respect of the property issued by the Council either informally or by virtue of the Council's wide range of statutory and regulatory powers. Such notices are issued principally under public health, housing or highways legislation. The Enquiry is **not** concerned with any of the following:

(i) Notices shown in the official certificate of search, since they create a local land charge and will be registered as such.
(ii) Notices issued under powers contained in the Town and Country Planning Act and dealt with in subsequent Part I Enquiries.
(iii) Notices served on owners of land after a compulsory purchase order has been made. These are notices to treat and as such are normally registrable as local land charges. They invite the owner concerned whose land is subject to a compulsory purchase order to put in a claim for compensation. The reference to Enquiry 13 directs the purchaser to inspect the reply to that Enquiry which concerns resolutions to make compulsory purchase orders.

CON 29: PART I STANDARD ENQUIRIES

Notices served on the property which this Enquiry is designed to reveal may be served under numerous Acts, the foremost of which will be the Public Health Act 1936, Housing Act 1985 and Highways Act 1980. Examples under each heading are as follows:

Public Health Act

(i) Notice requiring the carrying out of works to remedy an overflowing cesspool (s 50).
(ii) Notice requiring owner to remedy the condition of filthy or verminous premises by cleaning and disinfecting them (s 83).

Housing Act

(i) Repair notice requiring the carrying out of works on a house which is unfit for human habitation but which is capable of being rendered fit for human habitation at reasonable expense (s 189).
(ii) Repair notice requiring the carrying out of works on a house to bring it up to reasonable standard, the house not being unfit for human habitation (s 190).
(iii) Notice requiring the abatement of overcrowding of a house (s 338).

Highways Act

(i) Notice requiring occupier of a building to remove or alter a porch, shed, projecting window, wall or fence which has been erected against or in front of the building and is an obstruction to safe or convenient passage along the street (s 152).
(ii) Notice requiring occupier of land to lop or cut a hedge, tree or shrub where it overhangs the highway so as to cause a danger or obstruction (s 154).
(iii) Notice requiring removal of barbed wire from a fence where it is a nuisance to the highway users (s 164).
(iv) Notice requiring owners of premises fronting a private street to carry out urgent repairs to the street to prevent danger to traffic (s 230).

Further examples of notices affecting property which a Council has power to issue under environmental and safety legislation include:

Enquiry 5: Outstanding notices

Health and Safety at Work Act 1974

(i) Improvement notice issued by a health and safety inspector in respect of contraventions of statutory provisions relating to health and safety. Such notices will identify the breach of safety requirements and require remedial action to be taken (s 21).

(ii) Prohibition notice issued by an inspector in respect of activities being carried out involving a serious risk of personal injury. These notices direct the activities complained of to cease with immediate effect (s 22).

Food Safety Act 1990

(i) Improvement notice issued in respect of a food business for breach of regulations relating to the use of any process or treatment in the preparation of food or the observance of hygienic conditions (s 10).

(ii) Emergency prohibition notice served in respect of a food business where there is an imminent risk of injury to health.

Environmental Protection Act 1990

Notices requiring the abatement of a statutory nuisance, eg premises in such a state as to be prejudicial to health, animals kept in such a place as to be a nuisance, accumulations or deposits of refuse, dust etc (s 80).

The London Building Acts, with the exception of the provisions relating to the naming and numbering of streets, apply only to the inner London boroughs. Within those boroughs the construction of buildings was formerly governed by the London Building Acts and supplementary by-laws made by the now defunct Greater London Council. District surveyors employed by the Greater London Council supervised building works in much the same way as do building control officers elsewhere.

The Greater London Council also had duties under the London Building Acts relating to building near dangerous and noxious businesses, dwellings on low-lying land and means of fire escape.

In inner London, the London Borough Councils and Corporation of the City of London had responsibility for the control of dangerous and neglected structures.

CON 29: PART I STANDARD ENQUIRIES

When the Greater London Council was abolished in 1985, its functions under the London Building Acts and the duties of the district surveyors were transferred to the inner London boroughs and the Corporation of the City of London in respect of their areas.

The Building Regulations 1985 (as mentioned in the commentary on Enquiry 6: see page 40) now also apply to the inner London boroughs, and considerable amendment has been necessary to what remains of the London Building Acts.

The London Building Acts, however, remain in force in respect of the inner London boroughs which have regulatory functions and duties under those Acts in relation to the naming and numbering of streets and buildings, the construction of buildings (including roof drainage, fire precautions and the "uniting of two buildings into one"), temporary buildings and structures, neglected structures and the making of by-laws.

Examples of the "statutory or informal notices" which may have been issued by an Inner London Borough Council and which a reply to this Enquiry might be expected to reveal are as follows:

(a) Section 35 London Building Acts (Amendment) Act 1939
— Notice requiring owner of an old building occupied by a number of families or as a boarding house to provide proper and sufficient means of escape in the event of fire.
(b) Section 62 London Building Acts (Amendment) Act 1939
— Notice requiring owner or occupier of a certified dangerous structure to take it down or to repair or secure it.
(c) Section 88 London Building Acts (Amendment) Act 1939
— Notice of Irregularity served by district surveyor in respect of a building or structure which is being erected or constructed in contravention of the provisions of the Act requiring the builder to amend the irregularity within forty-eight hours.

The following is a list of the London Borough Councils (together with the City of London Corporation) divided into inner and outer status:

Enquiry 5: Outstanding notices

Inner London Authorities	*Outer London Authorities*
City of London	Barking & Dagenham
Camden	Barnet
Greenwich	Bexley
Hackney	Brent
Hammersmith & Fulham	Bromley
Islington	Croydon
Kensington & Chelsea	Ealing
Lambeth	Enfield
Lewisham	Haringey
Southwark	Harrow
Tower Hamlets	Havering
Wandsworth	Hillingdon
Westminster	Hounslow
	Kingston-upon-Thames
	Merton
	Newham
	Redbridge
	Richmond-upon-Thames
	Sutton
	Waltham Forest

Summary

Enquiry 5 asks whether any of these notices or other such notices under the Acts have been served on the premises the subject of the Enquiries. A purchaser will obviously prefer a negative answer.

Enquiry 6: Building Regulations

What proceedings have the Council authorised in respect of an infringement of the Building Regulations?

This Enquiry relates to breaches of the Building Regulations.

The Building Regulations 1985 are designed to control the carrying out of building work in the erection, extension or alteration of buildings. All building work must be carried out in compliance with the detailed requirements contained in Schedules to the Regulations, and with proper materials and in a workmanlike manner.

Builders or others intending to carry out building works are required to give certain notices and deposit certain building plans with the Council and obtain approval before work commences. Further notices must be given to the Council at specified stages in the progress of work, to enable the Council's officers to inspect.

The particular requirements of the Regulations are extremely detailed and cover matters under the following headings:

(A) Structure

Loading (requirements of dead, imposed and wind loads)
Ground movement (movements of the subsoil caused by swelling, shrinkage or freezing)

(B) Fire

Means of escape

Enquiry 6: Building Regulations

Internal fire spread (resistance to the spread of flames)
External fire spread (roof and external walls)

(C) Site preparation and resistance to moisture

Preparation of site (freedom from vegetable matter)
Dangerous and offensive substances
Subsoil drainage (ie to avoid the passage of ground moisture into the building)
Resistance to weather and ground moisture

(D) Toxic substances

Cavity insulation (prevention of permeation of toxic fumes)

(E) Resistance to the passage of sound

Airborne sound (walls and floors)

(F) Ventilation

Means of ventilation
Condensation

(G) Hygiene

Bathrooms
Hot water storage (to prevent water exceeding 100°C)
Sanitary conveniences and washing facilities

(H) Drainage and waste disposal

Foul water drainage
Cesspools, septic tanks and settlement tanks (access for emptying)
Rainwater drainage
Solid waste storage (access for removal)

(J) Heat-producing appliances

Air supply (ie to heat-producing appliances)
Discharge of products of combustion (ie to the outside air)
Protection of building (from risk of fire)

(K) Stairways, ramps and kerbs

Stairways and ramps (safe passage for users)
Protection from falling (by barriers, guards etc)
Vehicle barriers

(L) Conservation of fuel and power

Under s 35 of the Building Act 1984 (under which Act the Regulations are made), it is a *criminal offence* punishable by a magistrates' court to contravene provisions of the Building Regulations.

Summary

Enquiry 6 asks for details of proceedings that the Council has authorised to be taken against someone for contravention of the Building Regulations in respect of the premises searched against. A purchaser will prefer a negative answer: even though the purchaser will not be prosecuted for breaking the Regulations himself, a positive answer will indicate that all is not well with the property.

Enquiry 7: Planning applications and permissions

Applications and Decisions
7.1. *Please list –*
   (a) any entries in the Register of planning applications and permissions,
   (b) any applications, and decisions in respect of listed building consent and
   (c) any applications, and decisions in respect of conservation area consent.

Inspection and Copies
7.2. *If there are any entries:*
   (a) how can copies be obtained?
   (b) where can the Register be inspected?

This Enquiry relates to the register of planning applications which the Council is required to keep pursuant to s 69 of the Town and Country Planning Act, and where that register is to be kept. It also relates to applications for listed building consent and conservation area consent in respect of the property.

The Council, as local planning authority, must keep a register containing information relating to applications for planning permission, including information as to the manner in which the applications have been dealt with.

The register provides a public record of planning applications and decisions, and also gives the public notification of all applications that have been made.

CON 29: PART I STANDARD ENQUIRIES

The register is kept in two parts:

Part I contains a copy of every application for planning permission together with copies of plans and drawings submitted with them. Entries must be made in the register within fourteen days of the application being received by the Council. The Council's own proposals for development must also appear in this part of the register before they can be carried out. Applications for planning permission must remain in Part I until finally disposed of, ie granted or refused.

Part II is a permanent record of all applications for planning permission and the decisions taken by the Council on them.

The following matters must be entered in Part II of the register:

(i) a copy of the application and any plans and drawings submitted with it;
(ii) any directions given under the Town and Country Planning Act in respect of the application;
(iii) the decision of the Council and the date of that decision;
(iv) the date and effect of any appeal decision of the Secretary of State on the application;
(v) the date of any subsequent approval (such as approval of reserved matters, ie matters of detail such as materials to be used in construction, etc).

The Council must also keep, in this part of the register, details of any development it has decided to carry out itself. The register must include an index for reference purposes.

Summary

Enquiry 7.1.(a) asks for details of any entries relating to planning applications that have been made or any decisions of the Council or the Secretary of State recorded in either Part I or Part II of the register. A purchaser will want to know what applications have been made and whether they have been granted or refused. This will give him an idea of what use he may put the property to, and whether he is likely to be able to get planning permission for any development he is contemplating himself. Clearly, if the register shows a previous refusal, for example, of commercial development on housing land, this is likely to indicate that a further similar application will also be unsuccessful.

Enquiry 7: Planning applications and permissions

* * *

A listed building is a building of special architectural or historic interest which has been identified as such by the Secretary of State (sometimes on the advice of the Historic Buildings and Monuments Commission) and placed upon a list of such buildings in accordance with powers and duties of the Secretary of State now comprised in the Planning (Listed Buildings and Conservation Areas) Act 1990. The number of listed buildings in England and Wales is now approaching half a million.

Buildings may be listed either on account of their particular architectural or historic merit, or because of their relationship to other such buildings, and there may be particular features or characteristics which make the building worth listing either for itself or as part of a group of buildings. Once listed, any object or structure fixed to the building or within its curtilage should be treated as part of the building, so that, for instance, a garden wall surrounding a listed building will also be protected by the listing (if it was in existence before 1 July 1948).

Once the lists are compiled by the Secretary of State, they must be deposited with the Council for the area covering the buildings concerned and the details must be entered in the Register of Local Land Charges by the Council and appear in an Official Certificate of Search as such. Copies of the lists must also be kept available for public inspection at the Council offices, insofar as they relate to properties in its area.

There are two main categories of listed buildings:

- Grade I   buildings of exceptional interest. Only approximately 2% of all listed buildings fall into this category.
- Grade II buildings of special interest, covering the majority of listed buildings. Some particularly important buildings in this category may be classified Grade II*.

To be listed, a building must normally fall into one of the following classifications:

(i) Built before 1700 and surviving in more or less original condition.

CON 29: PART I STANDARD ENQUIRIES

(ii) Built between 1700 and 1840 (selection is necessary).
(iii) Built between 1840 and 1914 and of definite quality – the principal works of principal architects will be included.
(iv) Built between 1914 and 1939 and selected for its high quality.
(v) Built after 1939 and of outstanding quality.

The main consequences of a building being listed are that it will attract all the protection of the Planning (Listed Buildings and Conservation Areas) Act 1990. That is to say:

(a) Any person causing damage to a listed building may be prosecuted for this offence and ordered to pay a fine.
(b) Listed building consent will be required for the demolition or alteration of a listed building.
(c) Special listed building enforcement notices may be served by the Council (for which see commentary on Enquiry 8: Notices under Planning Acts).
(d) There are limitations on the permitted development rights under the Town and Country Planning General Development Order (see commentary on Enquiry 9: Directions restricting permitted development).

It is (b) above with which Enquiry 7.1.(b) is concerned.

Under s 7 of the Planning (Listed Buildings and Conservation Areas) Act 1990, if a person carries out any works for the demolition of a listed building or for its alteration or extension in any manner which would affect its character as a building of special architectural or historic interest, and these works have not been authorised, the person carrying out those works will be guilty of an offence and may be prosecuted for a fine or may be imprisoned. Works will only be authorised if:

(i) the Council or the Secretary of State has granted listed building consent and any conditions attached to the consent are complied with; and
(ii) in the case of demolition, notice of the proposal to demolish has been given to the Royal Commission on the Historical Monuments of England – in relation to Wales, the Royal Commission on Ancient and Historical Monuments in Wales – to give the Commission the opportunity to make a record of the building before it is demolished.

Enquiry 7: Planning applications and permissions

Application for listed building consent must be made to the Council as local planning authority containing sufficient details to identify the building, including plans and drawings sufficient to describe the proposed works. The Council then advertises the application in the local newspaper and displays a site notice on the building. The Council must also notify the Secretary of State (or the Historic Buildings and Monuments Commission if the building is in London).

The Council may grant listed building consent for the proposed works, and in so doing will have regard to the importance of the building, its architectural merit, its historical interest, its condition, the cost of repairing and maintaining it, and other factors. If listed building consent is refused, the person wishing to carry out the works has a right of appeal to the Secretary of State who may hold a public local inquiry into the matter and either confirm the Council's refusal or himself grant listed building consent, with or without conditions, having heard the evidence.

Summary

Enquiry 7.1.(b) asks for details of any applications and decisions in respect of listed building consent, including grants of such consent by the Secretary of State on appeal from the Council's refusal. If listed building consent has been granted, the purchaser will want to know full details, including any conditions which have been imposed on the consent, since carrying out work in breach of any of those conditions will render him liable to prosecution.

* * *

An outline of the provisions relating to conservation areas is to be found in the commentary on Enquiry 12: Pre-registration conservation area. The protection accorded to individual listed buildings by the provisions of the Planning (Listed Buildings and Conservation Areas) Act 1990 is extended, in modified form, to all buildings situated within a conservation area designated by the Council as local planning authority or the Secretary of State.

In particular, by virtue of s 74 of the Act, a building in a conservation area may not be demolished without the consent of the Council as local planning authority and such consent, if granted, is known as "conservation area consent". Application for consent must be made to the Council as local planning authority and be accompanied by details similar to those required in respect of a listed building consent application. Consent may be granted with or without conditions. Refusal of consent by the Council may be appealed to the Secretary of State. Contravention of the conditions attached to a conservation area consent renders the owner of the building liable to prosecution, imprisonment or fine.

Summary

Enquiry 7.1.(c) asks for details of any applications and decisions in respect of conservation area consent. If the property enquired about does not lie within a designated conservation area, this part of the Enquiry will be irrelevant. If conservation area consent has been granted, the purchaser will want to know full details, including any conditions which have been imposed on the consent, since carrying out demolition in breach of any of those conditions will render him liable to prosecution.

* * *

The register of planning applications and decisions must be kept at the office of the local planning authority, ie the Council offices. It is kept in addition to the register of enforcement and stop notices referred to in Enquiry 8 below. Although parts of the register may be kept at different offices convenient to the areas of land to which they relate, in practice the register will be kept at the Council offices which accommodate the planning department.

Summary

Enquiry 7.2.(a) asks where copies of entries on the register of planning applications and decisions, and copies of listed building or conservation area applications and decisions may be obtained. Since such documents are of a public nature, the Council will normally supply copies on request, but is not bound to do so free of charge. The Council has a degree of

Enquiry 7: Planning applications and permissions

copyright protection in supplying copies of documents in pursuance of its statutory obligation to keep a register.

Enquiry 7.2.(b) asks where the register can be inspected. Since it must be open to public inspection at all reasonable hours, a purchaser will want to be told where he can see it.

Enquiry 8: Notices under Planning Acts

Enforcement and Stop Notices
8.1.1. Please list any entries in the Register of enforcement notices and stop notices.
8.1.2. If there are any entries:
(a) how can copies be obtained?
(b) where can that Register be inspected?

Proposed Enforcement or Stop Notice
8.2. Except as shown in the Official Certificate of Search, or in reply to enquiry 8.1.1, has any enforcement notice, listed building enforcement notice or stop notice been authorised by the Council for issue or service (other than notices which have been withdrawn or quashed)?

Compliance with Enforcement Notices
8.3. If an enforcement notice or listed building enforcement notice has been served or issued, has it been complied with to the satisfaction of the Council?

Other Contravention Notices etc
8.4. Has the Council served, or resolved to serve, any other notice or proceedings relating to a contravention of planning control?

Listed Building Repairs Notices, etc.
8.5.1. To the knowledge of the Council, has the service of a repairs notice been authorised?

Enquiry 8: Notices under Planning Acts

8.5.2. If the Council have authorised the making of an order for the compulsory acquisition of a listed building, is a "minimum compensation" provision included, or to be included, in the order?

8.5.3. Have the Council authorised the service of a building preservation notice?

This Enquiry relates to breaches of planning control affecting the premises and action taken or proposed by the Council. With regard to listed buildings, the Enquiry is also concerned with the service of listed building enforcement notices, repairs notices and compulsory purchase orders by the Council for lack of repair, and building preservation notices served by the Council as an interim measure before the property becomes listed.

Under the Town and Country Planning Act 1990, planning permission issued by the Council is required for the carrying out of any development of land. Development, for these purposes, is defined to mean either:

(i) the carrying out of building, engineering, mining or other operations; or
(ii) the making of any material change in the use of any buildings or land.

Thus, for example, planning permission will be required before any building or other structure can be erected. In addition, planning permission will be required before the use to which any existing building is put can be changed (with certain exceptions) so that, for example, change of use of a building from house to shop will require planning permission.

If application for planning permission is duly made, it may be granted by the Council subject to conditions which must be complied with.

If a person carries out development, either by erecting a building or structure or by changing the use of an existing building or structure, without first obtaining planning permission, the Council may serve an enforcement notice on that person. The enforcement notice will require the person who has carried out the development, *or any other owner of the land in question,* to restore the land or buildings to the original condition, or to cease the unauthorised change of use, and it will give a prescribed time in which to comply with the notice. These notices are served under s 172 of the Town and Country Planning Act.

The recipient of an enforcement notice may appeal against its requirements to the Secretary of State; if he does so, no further action can be taken by the Council until the appeal is dealt with. If, at the appeal, the enforcement notice is upheld, the recipient of the notice will have to comply with it within the prescribed time, which may have been extended by the Secretary of State.

If the person on whom the notice was served fails to comply with it within the prescribed time, he may be prosecuted in the magistrates' court or Crown Court and may have to pay a substantial penalty or even go to prison.

Failure to comply with a condition attached to a valid planning permission, eg failure to provide a landscaping scheme within a prescribed time of development commencing, is enforceable by the Council in the same way, ie service of enforcement notice and, ultimately, prosecution.

In addition, the Council has powers under the 1990 Act to carry out whatever work is necessary to remedy the breach of planning control and to charge the costs of so doing to the offender, and this is in addition to the power to prosecute.

In certain circumstances it may be particularly important to stop the unauthorised development before the time allowed in the enforcement notice for compliance. In these cases the Council may serve a stop notice prohibiting the unauthorised development but must give at least three days' notice. There is no appeal against a stop notice but if the enforcement notice, which will have been served before the stop notice, is successfully appealed against, the Council may have to pay compensation to the recipient of both notices, so that service of a stop notice by a Council is rare and will have to be justified on its particular circumstances. Stop notices are served under s 183 of the Town and Country Planning Act.

Enforcement and stop notices will normally be shown in the Official Certificate of Search or in the register which the Council is obliged to keep by virtue of s 188 of the Town and Country Planning Act.

A notice may be withdrawn at any time before it comes into effect (the date upon which it comes into effect is specified in

Enquiry 8: Notices under Planning Acts

the notice) but after it has come into effect it cannot be withdrawn, even after it has been complied with.

A notice may be quashed by the Secretary of State on appeal, in which case it is of no effect.

Summary

Enquiry 8.1.1 asks for a list of any relevant entries of enforcement and stop notices in the register which the Council is required to keep under s 188 of the Town and Country Planning Act. Obviously a purchaser will desire a negative response, but if entries are revealed he will require full details, including effective dates for compliance with the requirements of any notices.

Enquiry 8.1.2 asks where the register of enforcement and stop notices may be inspected and how copies of entries can be obtained. Under s 188 it must be open for public inspection at all reasonable hours and will generally be kept within the planning department of the Council's offices. Since the register is public, copies of entries should be made available to the enquirer on request, but the Council may impose a charge for this service.

* * *

As mentioned in the commentary on Enquiry 7: Planning applications and permissions, the carrying out of the works for the demolition or alteration of a listed building without the benefit of listed building consent, or the carrying out of these works otherwise than in strict compliance with any conditions attached to such a consent, will render the person carrying out those works liable to a fine or imprisonment. However, prosecution will not of itself restore the listed building.

Under s 38 of the Planning (Listed Buildings and Conservation Areas) Act 1990, the Council as local planning authority may in these circumstances, and if it feels it expedient to do so, issue and serve a listed building enforcement notice, specifying the contravention complained of, and requiring steps to be taken to restore the building to its former state. If such restoration would not be practicable, the Council may specify other works which would alleviate the effect of the works which have been carried out.

53

A listed building enforcement notice may also be served to achieve compliance with conditions attached to a listed building consent.

The notice will be served on the owner and the occupier of the building, and any other person who has an interest in it.

The person on whom the notice is served may appeal to the Secretary of State against the notice on a number of grounds, including the ground that the works were urgently necessary in the interests of safety or health or the preservation of the building.

If an appeal is made, the effect of the notice is suspended until the Secretary of State has held an inquiry into the matter and made his decision.

If no appeal is brought, or if an appeal is brought and is unsuccessful (ie the listed building enforcement notice is confirmed), failure to comply with its requirements is an offence and the person on whom the notice is served may be fined.

Enforcement notices, listed building enforcement notices and stop notices are issued by the Council after a report has been made to the relevant committee and a resolution has been passed to take appropriate action.

Summary

Enquiry 8.2 asks whether any enforcement notices, listed building enforcement notices or stop notices have been authorised for service by the Council; it is designed to reveal to an intending purchaser decisions made by the Council to issue and serve enforcement and stop notices where these notices have not yet been served. Notices which have already been served should be revealed by the Official Certificate of Search and the register of enforcement and stop notices kept by the Council under s 188 of the Town and Country Planning Act. This part of the Enquiry asks about proposals or intentions to serve such notices. A purchaser will prefer a negative response since he may be required to comply with enforcement (or listed building enforcement) notices subsequently served on the property. A purchaser will probably be deterred from buying a property if there is a likelihood that one of these notices will be served. The purchaser will not, however, normally be interested in notices which have been withdrawn or quashed.

Enquiry 8: Notices under Planning Acts

* * *

If the breach of planning control complained of in an enforcement notice has been put right, ie the offending building or structure has been demolished or the use has reverted to an authorised use, no further action will be taken under the enforcement notice, but the notice will remain on the record.

Similarly, if a listed building enforcement notice has already been served (and therefore should have been revealed by the Official Certificate of Search), it may have been complied with to the satisfaction of the Council. The notice will not, in these circumstances, be removed from the Register of Local Land Charges, but proceedings under the notice for prosecution will not take place.

Summary

Enquiry 8.3 asks whether any enforcement notice or listed building enforcement notice served in respect of the property has been complied with. A purchaser will obviously prefer an affirmative reply and may not be deterred from buying the property if he can get this reassurance. The Council will normally only reply to this Enquiry, however, if its officers have had an opportunity to inspect the property since the notice was served. If a special inspection is required to enable the Council to reply to this part of the Enquiry, the Council may not be prepared to conduct such an inspection unless the purchaser pays for it.

* * *

The Planning and Compensation Bill (which, at the time of going to print, is proceeding through Parliament) introduces a new set of planning enforcement measures, and makes considerable changes to the system of enforcement, listed building enforcement and stop notices. The amendments to the current system are not noted here, but mention should be made of the proposed new "planning contravention notice" which Enquiry 8.4 is principally devised to reveal.

A planning contravention notice will be served by the Council, as local planning authority, where it appears that there has been a breach of planning control. It will be served on any owner or occupier of the land concerned (or anybody carrying out operations on it) and will require specified information to be provided. A time and place may be specified in such a notice at which the authority will consider an offer to apply for planning permission, to refrain from carrying out the activities, or to undertake remedial works. Representations to such a notice may be made in person. It will be an offence to fail to comply with the requirements of the notice.

Planning contravention notices will not take the place of enforcement notices but may supplement their effectiveness and generally speed up enforcement procedures.

A general power is proposed in the Bill by which a local planning authority will be entitled to apply to the court for an injunction restraining actual or potential breaches of planning control, whether or not other enforcement measures have been contemplated.

Summary

Enquiry 8.4 is designed to elicit information in connection with any proposed planning contravention notices, injunctive or other proceedings (including prosecution for breach of enforcement notices). An intending purchaser will clearly prefer a negative response, but should request full details if an affirmative reply is given.

* * *

Part 5 of this Enquiry relates to the service of repairs notices on owners of listed buildings and the compulsory purchase of such buildings by the Council for lack of repair. This part of the Enquiry will be relevant only if the property enquired about is revealed to be listed, and a survey of the property has shown it to be in a bad state of repair.

The Town and Country Planning Act does not impose obligations on an owner of property, even the owner of a listed building, to maintain it in good repair. However, the Council, as local planning authority, does have the following powers (now contained in ss 47–56 of the Planning (Listed Buildings and Conservation Areas) Act 1990) in relation to listed buildings which have been allowed to fall into a state of disrepair:

Enquiry 8: Notices under Planning Acts

(i) power to carry out works urgently necessary for the preservation of an *unoccupied* listed building on giving at least seven days' prior notification to the owner (s 54);

(ii) power to acquire, with compulsory purchase powers if necessary, any listed building in need of repair, subject, in the case of buildings which have been allowed to fall into disrepair deliberately for the purpose of justifying demolition and redevelopment of the site, to the payment of "minimum compensation" calculated on the basis that neither planning permission nor listed building consent would be granted except for maintaining the building in a proper state of repair (ss 47 and 50).

The procedure contained in ss 47 and 48 of the Planning (Listed Buildings and Conservation Areas) Act 1990 enables a Council compulsorily to acquire listed buildings in need of repair. The procedures are really designed to encourage preservation of these buildings and compulsory acquisition by the Council will only be invoked as a last resort.

The first step is the service of a repairs notice under s 48. The compulsory purchase of a listed building under s 47 (next discussed) cannot proceed unless this notice has been served. It must be served on the owner of a listed building at least two months before s 47 compulsory purchase powers are invoked. The repairs notice must specify the works which it is considered are reasonably necessary for the proper preservation of the building in question. The notice may not require the complete restoration of the building with all its features of architectural and historic interest (it may not have been in this condition for many years). Only those works reasonably necessary to preserve the building may be required.

The repairs notice must also explain to the owner the effect of the provisions of the Act relating to compulsory purchase. The notice in effect gives the owner an opportunity to put the building into a state of repair, before the Council goes one step further and commences the compulsory purchase procedure.

The compulsory purchase of listed buildings in disrepair may be pursued by the Council, as local planning authority, or the

Secretary of State, who originally compiles the lists of listed buildings, or, if the building is in Greater London, the Historic Buildings and Monuments Commission. Each of these may serve a listed building repairs notice under s 48.

Summary

Enquiry 8.5.1 asks whether the Council is aware of any listed building repairs notices which have been authorised. The Enquiry should therefore reveal not merely notices that have been served by the Council, but also notices which the Council, the Secretary of State or the Historic Buildings and Monuments Commission have *authorised to be served*. The Council should be aware of any such notices it has itself authorised to be served but may not be aware as yet of any authorised to be served by the Secretary of State or the Commission. A purchaser will obviously prefer a negative response, since otherwise there will be a likelihood that the property will be compulsorily purchased if it is not put into order without delay. A prudent purchaser will make further enquiries of the Secretary of State or the Commission if the property is listed and in a state of disrepair, since a negative response here will not necessarily mean that no such notices have been authorised to be served, merely that the Council is not aware of any.

* * *

Once the repairs notice has been served, if it appears to the Secretary of State that reasonable steps are still not being taken for properly preserving the property, he may authorise the Council for the district in which it is situated (or the Historic Buildings and Monuments Commission if the property is in London) to acquire the property compulsorily and any land adjacent to it which is considered necessary for preserving the building or its amenities. The Council makes and submits to the Secretary of State a compulsory purchase order, and if the Secretary of State is satisfied that this is a necessary course of action to make provision for the preservation of the building, he will confirm the order.

Any owner or other person having an interest in the building may apply to a magistrates' court for an order staying proceedings under the compulsory purchase order and if the

Enquiry 8: Notices under Planning Acts

court is satisfied that reasonable steps have been taken for properly preserving the building, the court may make such an order.

Compensation will be due and payable to the owner of a listed building by the Council if it uses these compulsory purchase powers, and the compensation will generally amount to the market value of the property concerned. Under s 49 of the Act, in assessing the compensation, any depreciation in value attributable to the possible restriction on alteration or extension of the building due to its being listed must be disregarded, so that the owner should generally obtain open market value (bearing in mind the property's state of disrepair) without regard to the restrictions which listing imposes.

However, by virtue of s 50, where the Council proposing to exercise these compulsory purchase powers is satisfied that the building has been *deliberately* allowed to fall into disrepair for the purpose of justifying its demolition and redevelopment, the Council may include in the compulsory purchase order a direction for "minimum compensation". This provision is aimed at discouraging owners of listed buildings from deliberately allowing the buildings to fall into disrepair so that the property can be demolished and redeveloped. The effect of a "minimum compensation" direction is that compensation payable for the building on its compulsory purchase will be assessed on the basis that neither planning permission nor listed building consent would be granted for any works except to restore the building to a proper state of repair and so maintain it. Such a direction will obviously have a considerable effect on the compensation which the owner will recover and this can be seen as a form of punishment for deliberately allowing the property to deteriorate.

There is a right of appeal against the decision to insert a "minimum compensation" provision in the compulsory purchase order. The appeal is to the magistrates' court and if it can be shown to the court that the building has not been allowed to fall into disrepair deliberately, the magistrates may order the provision not to be included so that proper compensation will be paid.

CON 29: PART I STANDARD ENQUIRIES

Summary

Enquiry 8.5.2 asks whether a "minimum compensation" provision has been or is intended to be included in a compulsory purchase order authorised to be made by the Council for the compulsory purchase of the property. A purchaser who has not been dissuaded from buying the property by the fact that it is to be subjected to compulsory purchase will prefer a negative response to this part of the Enquiry so that he may expect full compensation. If an affirmative reply is forthcoming, this will substantially affect the price he will be willing to pay.

* * *

The final part of this Enquiry relates to building preservation notices served by the Council as an interim measure to the property becoming a listed building.

A brief résumé of the criteria for listing buildings was given in the commentary on Enquiry 7: Planning applications and permissions.

Listed buildings are buildings of special architectural or historic interest which appear on lists compiled by the Secretary of State and deposited with the Council. Once the lists are deposited with the Council, they are local land charges and any building appearing on the list will appear in the Register as such. The fact that a building is listed will therefore appear in the Official Certificate of Search.

Buildings are listed either on account of their particular architectural or historic merit, or because of their relationship to other such buildings, and there may be particular features or characteristics which make the building worth listing either for itself or as part of a group of buildings.

Once listed, any object or structure fixed to the building or forming part of the curtilage must be treated as part of the building so that, for instance, a garden wall surrounding a listed building will also be protected by the listing (provided it was in existence on 1 July 1948).

Although the owner and occupier of a building which is listed must be informed of the fact, he need not be consulted. The Secretary of State is obliged to consult persons with special knowledge of, or interest in, such buildings, but is not obliged to consult the owner himself.

Enquiry 8: Notices under Planning Acts

The Secretary of State must keep the lists open and available for public inspection, and the Council must also keep available for public inspection any portion of the lists relating to properties in its area.

The consequences of a building being listed are briefly:

(i) Any person causing damage to a listed building may be prosecuted for this offence and ordered to pay a fine. Failure, after having been convicted, to prevent further damage, may result in a daily penalty being imposed by the court.
(ii) Listed building consent will be required for the demolition or alteration of a listed building. These were discussed in the commentary on Enquiry 7 above.
(iii) Special listed building enforcement notices may be served by the Council. These were discussed earlier in this commentary.

It will be seen that the initiative to compile these lists of buildings of special architectural or historic importance is taken by the Secretary of State. The Council cannot impose listed building status itself; it merely acts as a registering authority, receiving the lists, entering the details on the Register of Local Land Charges, notifying the owners and occupiers on behalf of the Secretary of State, and revealing the entries in the replies to official searches of the Register.

However, where a building is not listed by the Secretary of State, but it appears to the Council as local planning authority that, due to its special architectural or historic interest it ought to be listed *and* it is threatened with demolition or alteration, the Council may serve on the owner and occupier a building preservation notice. This has the effect of imposing the same protection as listed building status for a maximum period of six months.

The notice must either be served on the owner and occupier or, in a case of urgency, by fixing it conspicuously to the building.

The conditions which must be fulfilled before the Council may serve a building preservation notice are as follows:

(i) the building must *not* already be listed (otherwise the listed building protection would apply anyway);
(ii) it must, in the opinion of the Council as local planning authority, be of special architectural or historic interest;

(iii) it must be threatened with demolition or alteration. It will be recalled that, in normal circumstances, planning permission is not required for the demolition of a building. If it appears to the Council that a building of special architectural or historic interest is about to be demolished, it must act quickly with the service of a building preservation notice.

During the period of six months through which the building preservation notice lasts, the Council may request the Secretary of State to include the building concerned in one of the lists of listed buildings. If the Secretary of State agrees to do so, or notifies the Council that he does not intend to include it, then the building preservation notice ceases to have any effect. Thus the temporary protection afforded by the notice ceases once the Secretary of State has made his decision. The building will then either have the protection of full listed building status, if the Secretary of State has included it in a list, or cease to have any special protection at all, if the Secretary of State has decided not to include it in a list.

If the Secretary of State decides not to include the building in a list, a further building preservation notice cannot be served for at least twelve months. Furthermore, the Council may have to pay the owner compensation for any loss or damage caused by service of the building preservation notice if it has been unsuccessful, ie if the Council's attempts to have the building listed have failed. This may occur, for example, if the owner has entered into a contract with a demolition firm which then has to be breached by the owner since he is prevented from demolishing the building.

Summary

Enquiry 8.5.3 asks whether the Council has authorised the service of a building preservation notice in respect of the property, ie whether it has decided to attempt to have the building listed and to protect it in the meantime.

A purchaser will normally prefer a negative response: otherwise unless he can demolish the building or carry out the alterations he desires before the notice is actually served (and remember it may be served in urgent cases by affixing it to the property), there is a possibility that the building will be listed

Enquiry 8: Notices under Planning Acts

and the owner will then be substantially prevented from interfering with the property in the future. If the owner does demolish the building in contravention of the building preservation notice, he may be prosecuted for a substantial fine.

Within London, the Historic Buildings and Monuments Commission for England has the same powers to issue building preservation notices as does a London Borough Council, and for the purposes of such notices the Commission has the same functions as the London Borough Council acting as local planning authority.

If the property is situated in a London borough, it may be the subject of a building preservation notice issued by the Historic Buildings and Monuments Commission, and since a reply given by the Council will not reveal such a notice, a prudent purchaser should make separate enquiries of the Commission if there is any likelihood of such a notice being issued.

Enquiry 9: Directions restricting permitted development

Except as shown in the Official Certificate of Search, have the Council resolved to make a direction to restrict permitted development?

This Enquiry relates to permitted development under the General Development Order and restriction of that development.

As mentioned in the commentary on Enquiry 8 above, under the Town and Country Planning Act planning permission issued by the Council is necessary before any development of land within the area of the Council can take place, and for these purposes development means the carrying out of building, engineering, mining or other operations or the making of any material change in the use of buildings or land.

The exception to this general rule is the Town and Country Planning General Development Order 1988 which lists classes of development which may be carried out as if they had permission granted by the Council, that is to say these specified classes of development have permitted development rights, and application to the Council for permission is not necessary.

The General Development Order is extremely detailed but basically it defines some seventy-six classes of development which enjoy permitted development rights. Some of the more important or commonly used of these classes are as follows:

Enquiry 9: Directions restricting permitted development

Development within the curtilage of a dwellinghouse

eg (i) the enlargement of a dwellinghouse by not more than 70 cu m (or 15%);
 (ii) the erectionof a porch so long as the floor area is not more than 3 sq m;
 (iii) the installation of satellite antennae not exceeding 90 cm in size;
 (iv) the erection of sheds for poultry keeping;
 (v) the construction of hardstanding for vehicles;
 (vi) the erection of an oil storage tank for domestic heating not exceeding 3,500 litres.

Minor operations

eg (i) erection of fences, gates and walls not exceeding 2 m (1 m if abutting a highway);
 (ii) painting the exterior of a building.

Temporary uses

eg the use of land for any purpose except as a caravan site for not more than 28 days in any one year (14 days for markets and motor-car and motor-cycle racing).

Agricultural buildings

eg erection of agricultural buildings such as barns etc for use in agriculture.

Development by local authority

eg the carrying out of works for the maintenance or improvement of highways.

Any of the above classes of development and the other classes mentioned in the General Development Order will not need planning permission, provided they are carried out within the limitations imposed by the order. Permission has been granted generally for these classes by the order.

However, under Article 4 of the order, the Council as local planning authority, or the Secretary of State, may effectively take away the permitted development rights within a specified area. This they do by making an Article 4 direction. The direction is generally made by the Council and approved or modified by the Secretary of State. Once in force, any property within the area specified in the direction will no longer enjoy the permitted development rights granted it by the General Development Order, so that development of the specified kind can only proceed once planning permission for it has been applied for and granted in the usual way. For example, the erection of a barn on an agricultural holding will normally be permitted by the General Development Order. If, however, the Council makes an Article 4 direction removing within a particular agricultural area the permitted development rights granted in Part 6 of the Schedule to the order (agricultural buildings and operations), then the erection of such a barn will require specific planning permission, which of course the Council may refuse to grant.

Article 4 directions, once made by the Council and approved by the Secretary of State are registrable as local land charges and will therefore appear in the Official Certificate of Search.

Before the direction can be made, the Council will pass a resolution to make one.

Summary

Enquiry 9 asks whether the Council has decided to make an Article 4 direction removing permitted development rights of any particular class in the area which includes the property. The reply will reveal decisions to make such orders which have not yet been made. A purchaser will normally prefer a negative reply, but if the reply is affirmative he will certainly want to know whether the proposed direction will affect the use to which he wishes to put his property or any development he is likely to want to carry out.

Enquiry 10: Orders under Planning Acts

Revocation Orders etc.
10.1. *Except as shown in the Official Certificate of Search, have the Council resolved to make any Orders revoking or modifying any planning permission or discontinuing an existing planning use?*

Tree Preservation Order
10.2. *Except as shown in the Official Certificate of Search, have the Council resolved to make any Tree Preservation Orders?*

This Enquiry concerns the Council's powers under the Town and Country Planning Act to revoke planning permissions (s 97), to discontinue the authorised use of land (s 102), and to make tree preservation orders (s 198).

1. Revocation and modification orders

Once planning permission has been granted by the Council for a development, whether it be for the erection of buildings or for a change of use of existing land or buildings, that planning permission attaches to the land and for the benefit of any person who is for the time being the owner of the land or building, and it is often the case that the planning permission is not exercised by the original applicant. Land or buildings may be sold with the benefit of the planning permission once granted.

However, in exceptional circumstances, the Council may make an order revoking or modifying planning permission after it has been granted. If the planning permission is revoked in this way it is no longer of any effect and the buildings can no longer be erected or the change of use be put into effect. Orders made by the Council must normally be confirmed by the Secretary of State unless they are not opposed. Normally, however, they will be opposed and can only be confirmed by the Secretary of State after he has held a public local inquiry into the objections.

A Council can only make an order revoking or modifying a planning permission before building operations authorised by the planning permission have been *completed* or *before* any change of use authorised by the planning permission has taken place.

Two further points on revocation or modification orders are that:

(a) compensation may be payable to the owner of the land affected by the order for loss of the planning permission, and this may amount to a considerable sum; and
(b) in certain circumstances the owner of the land or building may be able to serve on the Council a purchase notice requiring the Council to buy the land the subject of the revocation or modification order.

It will be seen that Councils only use this power in exceptional circumstances, since the consequences could be very expensive.

2. Discontinuance orders

The power under s 97 (revocation or modification orders) relates to existing planning permissions and must be used by the Council before the building operations have been completed or the change of use has taken place. Discontinuance orders under s 102 may be made by the Council requiring the discontinuance of any use of land (or the imposition of conditions on its future use for any particular purpose) or indeed the removal or alteration of any buildings, even after they have been completed and may have been used or occupied quite lawfully for many years.

If it appears to the Council as local planning authority that it is in the best interests of the proper planning of the area, including the best interests of public amenity, the Council may make a discontinuance order under s 102.

Enquiry 10: Orders under Planning Acts

Once again, these orders must be confirmed by the Secretary of State and if there are objections, as there almost always will be, a public local inquiry must be held to enable the objectors to state their case.

If people are, as a result of an order under this section, required to leave their houses, the Council must normally rehouse them.

Compensation must be paid to the owner of the land if a discontinuance order is made, and this will amount to the sum by which the value of the land has depreciated as a result of the order.

Any person who breaches the terms of a discontinuance order may be prosecuted for this offence and may be liable to a substantial fine.

Summary

Enquiry 10.1 asks whether the Council has decided to make any revocation, modification or discontinuance orders which, when made, will affect the land or buildings which are the subject of the Enquiries. Orders which have already been made will be revealed by the Official Certificate of Search. A purchaser will prefer a negative reply since he will want to know that there is no doubt about his ability to use the land and buildings for the purposes for which he is buying them. If this part of the Enquiry reveals an intention by the Council to make one of these orders, the purchaser should seek full details.

* * *

3. Tree preservation orders

Councils have powers to preserve and protect trees or woodlands in their area, and in particular they may make orders, under s 198 of the Town and Country Planning Act, prohibiting the cutting down, topping, lopping, uprooting or causing wilful damage to particular trees or woodlands. The order made by the Council may require any person who wishes to interfere with protected trees to obtain consent from the Council before so doing.

These orders are made by the Council and although notice is first served on the owner of the land on which the trees grow, and objections must be taken into account before the order is confirmed, the Secretary of State's approval is no longer required so that the making of these orders (TPOs) is completely within the control of the Council.

Trees which are dying or dead or which have become dangerous may be uprooted without consent, but with this exception, where any tree protected by a TPO is removed or uprooted or destroyed, the person causing the damage or removing or destroying the tree may be prosecuted in the magistrates' court or Crown Court and fined a sum which may equal twice the value of the tree, or £2,000, whichever is the greater. Furthermore, the owner of the land may be required to plant another tree of an appropriate size and species as soon as reasonably practicable.

Revocation, modification, discontinuance and tree preservation orders are registrable in the Local Land Charges Register, and if made and confirmed, should be revealed on the Official Certificate of Search. However, before they are made, the Council must consider the circumstances and pass a resolution to make them.

Summary

Enquiry 10.2 asks whether the Council has decided to make any tree preservation orders which when made will affect the land or buildings which are the subject of the Enquiries. A purchaser will prefer a negative reply since he will normally not want to be burdened with the obligation to preserve trees. If an affirmative response is given, the purchaser should request full details of the trees proposed to be protected by the order; a physical inspection of the property is advisable to check on the existence and condition of the trees in question.

Enquiry 11: Compensation for planning decisions

What compensation has been paid by the Council under s.114 of the T&CP Act 1990 for planning decisions restricting development other than new development?

This Enquiry asks about compensation paid by the Council as a result of the imposition of conditions on a planning permission.

Section 114 compensation provisions are of very limited application.

The Town and Country Planning Act lists six types of development for which if the Secretary of State on appeal refuses planning permission, or grants planning permission subject to conditions, then compensation may be payable by the Council if the value of the land is reduced by the refusal of planning permission or the imposition of conditions attached to the permission. To qualify for this compensation the person wishing to develop the land must show that:

(i) an application for permission has been made to the Council and refused;
(ii) an appeal has been made to the Secretary of State against the Council's decision and the Secretary of State has refused to grant the permission or has granted it subject to conditions;
(iii) the value of the land is lessened by that refusal or by the conditions imposed; and
(iv) the application was for one of the six specified types of development listed in the Act.

The six types of development concerned are as follows:

(i) The enlargement or improvement of a building in existence on 1 July 1948, or any building substituted for a building which was in existence before that date but was demolished or destroyed after 7 January 1937, provided the cubic content of the original building is not increased by more than one tenth or 1750 cubic feet, whichever is the greater (dwellinghouses), or by more than one tenth for other buildings.

(ii) The carrying out of building for agricultural or forestry purposes on land which was agricultural or forestry land in 1948.

(iii) The working of minerals on land occupied with agricultural land, provided the minerals are needed for use on the agricultural land, eg for fertilizers or for the repair of agricultural buildings.

(iv) The use of a building for a purpose falling within the same general class of use to which the land was put in 1948.

(v) Where part of a building or the land was, in 1948, used for a particular purpose, the use for the same purpose of an additional part not exceeding one tenth of the original cubic content.

(vi) Where any land was, in 1948, comprised in a site used for the dumping of waste materials or refuse in connection with the working of minerals, the use for the same purpose of any additional part of the land which is required in connection with the working of minerals.

If the person wishing to develop the land wants to claim compensation from the Council for his inability to develop it as a result of the refusal of planning permission, he must make his claim within six months of the refusal.

Summary

Enquiry 11 simply asks whether compensation claimed under s 114 in the above circumstances has been paid by the Council. The purchaser will want a factual answer. A negative reply will be usual since the circumstances giving rise to compensation under this section are limited. However a positive reply, that is to say that compensation has been paid, will not

Enquiry 11: Compensation for planning decisions

prevent a purchaser from claiming further compensation provided he goes through the procedure of applying for planning permission, getting refused, and appealing to the Secretary of State, etc.

Enquiry 12: Pre-registration conservation area

Except as shown in the Official Certificate of Search, is the area a conservation area?

This Enquiry relates to conservation areas designated before 31 August 1974. Conservation areas designated after that date are local land charges and will be revealed in the Official Certificate of Search. The Enquiry also relates to areas designated by resolution of the Council as conservation areas but which have not, as yet, been registered in the Register of Local Land Charges.

Conservation areas are designated by Councils as local planning authorities, and they are areas of special architectural or historic interest which the Council considers desirable to preserve or enhance the character or appearance. It is the preservation of areas, as distinct from individual buildings, which s 69 of the Planning (Listed Buildings and Conservation Areas) Act 1990 is designed to provide for.

Conservation areas may be enlarged or reduced by the Council from time to time and whenever a Council designates a conservation area or enlarges or reduces it, it must notify the Secretary of State. The Council must also publicise the making or alteration of a conservation area in the London Gazette and the local newspaper.

The effects of a property lying within a designated conservation area can be summarised as follows:

(i) In general no building within the conservation area may be demolished without the consent of the Council – consent for demolition of buildings (other than listed buildings) not lying within conservation areas is generally not required.
(ii) Trees within conservation areas have very similar protection to those covered by tree preservation orders so that they cannot be cut down, uprooted, topped, lopped or destroyed or damaged without the consent of the Council, and any person who does damage such a tree may be prosecuted for a fine (see Enquiry 10 above).
(iii) The Council is under a duty to consider and publish proposals for the preservation and enhancement of the area.
(iv) Any applications for planning permission within the area for development which would affect the character or appearance of the conservation area must be given special publicity, and any objections to the proposed development must be taken into account by the Council before the application can be properly determined and permission given.
(v) Permitted development rights under the General Development Order (see Enquiry 9) and the right to display certain types of illuminated advertisement under the Town and Country Planning (Control of Advertisement) Regulations (see Enquiry 21) are either limited or excluded.

Summary

Enquiry 12 asks whether the property lies within one of these conservation areas, either recently designated by resolution of the Council and not yet registered in the Local Land Charges Register or designated before 31 August 1974. If it lies within a conservation area designated later than that date, this should be revealed in the Official Certificate of Search since such later conservation areas are local land charges.

A purchaser will want to know whether the property lies within a conservation area or not but whether he will prefer a negative or an affirmative reply will depend on the circumstances. There are advantages of a property lying within such an area – the area will be preserved and possibly enhanced in its architectural or historic context. There are also disadvantages — demolition and many classes of alteration to the premises may not be allowed, and this may be important to a prospective developer.

Enquiry 13: Compulsory purchase

Except as shown in the Official Certificate of Search, have the Council made any order (whether or not confirmed by the appropriate Secretary of State) or passed any resolution for compulsory acquisition which is still capable of being implemented?

This Enquiry relates to the use by Councils of their compulsory purchase powers.

As a statutory authority charged with the performance of a wide variety of functions, a Council has the power to purchase property compulsorily under a range of enactments for different purposes.

The *procedure* for compulsory purchase is contained largely in the Acquisition of Land Act 1981 and the Compulsory Purchase Act 1965, but the actual *power* to purchase land compulsorily for a particular purpose will be contained in legislation relevant to that purpose, eg Housing Acts, Highways Acts, Town and Country Planning Act.

In brief, the procedure is that the Council must first pass a resolution to acquire land for a specific purpose. The Council must then draft a compulsory purchase order and advertise it. The compulsory purchase order is then made (ie sealed and dated) and forwarded to the Secretary of State for confirmation. If there are no objections, the Secretary of State may confirm the order as unopposed. If there are objections the Secretary of State must generally arrange for a public local inquiry into those objections at which the case for the Council and the case for the objectors will be put. In due course the Secretary of State will decide whether the compulsory purchase order should be confirmed or not.

If the order is confirmed, the Council will serve upon the owners of the land in question a notice to treat, that is a notice inviting the owners to submit a claim for compensation based upon the value of the land to be purchased. Alternatively the Council may make a vesting declaration which passes ownership of the land direct to the Council, subject to appropriate compensation being paid. Notices to treat and the like are registrable in the Register of Local Land Charges.

A footnote to Form CON 29 acts as a warning to its users that other authorities have compulsory purchase powers and should be consulted if there is any question that compulsory purchase may be a threat to the property. Authorities other than District (or London Borough) Councils having compulsory purchase powers include the following:

(i) Central Government Departments
(ii) Statutory undertakers
(iii) Railway authorities
(iv) Road and transport authorities
(v) County Councils
(vi) Water transport authorities
(vii) Electricity, gas or hydraulic power undertakers
(viii) British Airports Authority
(ix) Civil Aviation Authority
(x) Post Office
(xi) British Telecom

Summary

Enquiry 13 asks whether any compulsory purchase order, either confirmed or not yet confirmed, has been made by the Council, or whether the Council has passed any resolution to make one. A purchaser will normally prefer a negative reply and indeed an affirmative reply will normally deter a purchaser from proceeding with the purchase. An affirmative reply will be given in any case where any part of the premises concerned is the subject of a proposed or actual compulsory purchase order.

Enquiry 14: Areas designated under Housing Acts etc

Clearance
14.1. Has any programme of clearance for the area been –
(a) submitted to the Department of the Environment, or
(b) resolved to be submitted, or
(c) otherwise adopted by resolution of the Council?

Housing
14.2. Except as shown in the Official Certificate of Search, have the Council resolved to define the area as designated for a purpose under the Housing Acts? If so, please specify the purpose.

This Enquiry relates to clearance areas, general improvement areas and housing action areas designated, or proposed for designation, which may affect the property enquired about.

Clearance areas are areas which are to be cleared of *all* buildings, and they are areas which predominantly consist of houses which are unfit for human habitation or are otherwise dangerous or injurious to the health of the inhabitants of the area.

Clearance areas are declared under s 289 of the Housing Act 1985. The Council, as local housing authority, must declare an area to be a clearance area if it is satisfied that the houses in the area are unfit for human habitation or, by reason of their bad arrangement, they are dangerous or injurious to health, and that the most satisfactory method of dealing with conditions in the area would be demolition of all of the buildings.

Before declaring a clearance area, the Council must first serve notice of its intention on the owners of all the buildings affected and publish notice of intention in the local newspapers. The notices must invite representations from interested persons and give at least 28 days for response. All representations must be considered by the Council before it decides to declare a clearance area. Once it has taken the decision to declare a clearance area, the Council must define it on a map so as to exclude from it buildings which are not unfit for human habitation, and then pass a resolution declaring the defined area as a clearance area.

The Council may have to arrange for the rehousing of displaced persons, and it must make suitable arrangements before declaring the clearance area. It must also ensure that sufficient financial resources are available to the Council to provide for this rehousing obligation.

The Council then sends to the Secretary of State a copy of the resolution it has made declaring the clearance area, together with a statement of the number of persons occupying the buildings comprised in the clearance area.

Any land already in a general improvement area (see below) must be excluded from the clearance area.

Once the clearance area has been declared, the Council must proceed to clear it by purchasing the land comprised in the area and demolishing the buildings. This it must either do by agreement with the owners of the land concerned, or by use of compulsory purchase powers (and the use of these powers must of course be confirmed, if necessary after a public local inquiry, by the Secretary of State).

The Council may also purchase land surrounded by the clearance area or adjoining it, if such land is reasonably necessary for the satisfactory development or use of the area as a whole.

Summary

Enquiry 14.1 asks whether the property lies within a clearance area which has been adopted by the Council or submitted to the Secretary of State or is about to be so submitted.

Enquiry 14: Areas designated under Housing Acts etc

An affirmative response to any part of this Enquiry will deter most purchasers from proceeding with the purchase, since although they will be able to recover compensation from the Council for a subsequent purchase by the Council, they will not be able to use the building concerned for any useful purpose.

* * *

General improvement areas (GIAs) also concern areas which predominantly consist of residential properties but here the accent is on *improvement* rather than *demolition and clearance.*

General improvement areas are declared under s 253 of the Housing Act 1985.

In deciding whether to declare a GIA, a Council, as local housing authority, first considers a report submitted to it about the area concerned, and if it is satisfied that the living conditions in that area can be improved by the improvement of amenities of the area or of the dwellings in it, or both, and that such improvement may be effected or assisted by the exercise of its powers under s 253, it then causes the area to be defined on a map and declares it to be a GIA.

A GIA cannot include land defined as a clearance area (see above) or land defined as a housing action area (see below).

Once declared by the Council as a GIA, the GIA must be publicised. The Council must publish a notice in the local newspaper identifying the area and specifying a place where the resolution and map may be inspected (generally the Council offices). Persons owning or occupying properties within the GIA must also be personally notified.

A copy of the resolution of the Council, the map and the report concerning the GIA are then sent to the Secretary of State, together with a statement of the number of dwellings comprised in the GIA.

Once the GIA has been declared and published, the Council may put improvements of the area into effect either by carrying out works on land it already owns or by assisting owners to carry out improvements by giving them grants or loans. The Council can also agree to buy land within the GIA, or use its compulsory purchase powers, but the latter will be rare, since the Council's intentions in declaring a GIA are generally to seek improvements by agreement.

The powers of the Council in connection with GIAs are not confined to improvements to housing. The Council may use powers to extinguish highway rights and thus make attractive pedestrian areas in certain cases.

The Council may receive contributions from the Secretary of State towards its expenditure incurred in the improvement of a GIA.

No new GIAs may be declared after 1 April 1990. By virtue of the Local Government and Housing Act 1989, all existing GIAs ceased on 1 April 1991, although they may still appear on the register. From 1 April 1991, GIAs will be replaced by renewal areas declared under s 89 of the Local Government and Housing Act 1989.

Housing Action Areas (HAAs) are designed to deal specifically with areas of poor housing, generally within the inner cities. Councils, as local housing authorities, have more extensive powers within HAAs and a higher level of grant aid is available to those availing themselves of the opportunity.

HAAs are concerned with areas consisting primarily of housing accommodation. The Council, in reliance upon a report of its officers and other relevant information, may declare by resolution an area defined on a map as an HAA. Before declaring such an area an HAA, the Council must be satisfied that living conditions in the area are unsatisfactory and can most effectively be dealt with by declaring an HAA so as to improve standards of housing accommodation, its proper and effective management, and the general well-being of the residents. In particular, Councils are required to have regard to both physical conditions (lack of standard amenities, bad layout, cramped back yards and other adverse features) and social conditions (shared cooking facilities, shared bath and water closet).

Once declared by resolution of the Council, publicity must be given to the HAA in the local press and by notification of those residing in or owning property in the area. The opportunity must be given to make representations regarding action to be taken in the HAA. A copy of the resolution, map and report, and a statement of the number of dwellings affected must be forwarded to the Secretary of State who

Enquiry 14: Areas designated under Housing Acts etc

may, within 28 days of receipt, notify the Council that the area declared to be an HAA is no longer to be such an area, or he may exclude land from the defined area. If the Secretary of State takes no action, the HAA may be taken to be confirmed.

Powers of the Council, as local housing authority, within an HAA, include the following:

(a) to acquire, by agreement or with compulsory purchase powers, housing accommodation;
(b) to provide housing accommodation by construction, conversion or improvement of buildings;
(c) to improve, repair and manage housing accommodation;
(d) to provide furniture, fittings or services in connection with housing;
(e) to carry out environmental works on land owned by the Council;
(f) to make grants for the carrying out of environmental works (ie works other than to the interior of the housing accommodation), and the provision of materials for such works.

A landlord of property within an HAA must notify the Council within 7 days of service of any notice to quit on his tenant, or not less than 4 weeks before any tenancy is due to expire by effluxion of time.

HAAs have had a normal life span of 5 years, subject to earlier termination or extension. However, as with GIAs, no new HAAs may be declared after 1 April 1990, and those with more than 2 years to run on that date ceased on 1 April 1991, although they may still appear on the register. From 1 April 1991 HAAs will be replaced by renewal areas declared under s 89 of the Local Government and Housing Act 1989.

Summary

Enquiry 14.2 is designed to reveal whether or not the property is situated within an area which is to be defined and declared as a general improvement area, housing action area, or renewal area.

The Official Certificate of Search may reveal such an area if it has already been declared, but this Enquiry is designed to reveal whether or not such an area is proposed to be declared which includes the property. Generally a purchaser will be happy with an affirmative response since grants may be available to him, quite apart from any improvement grants to which he might have been entitled. Declaration of such an area will also indicate the Council's intention generally to upgrade the appearance and amenity of the area. Landlords of properties within housing action areas should be aware of their duty to notify the Council when they serve any notices to quit or before fixed term tenancies expire by effluxion of time.

Enquiry 15: Smoke control order

Except as shown in the Official Certificate of Search, have the Council made a smoke control order or resolved to make or vary a smoke control order for the area?

This Enquiry concerns proposals by the Council to make or vary a smoke control order affecting the property. It deals with the regime of smoke control introduced by the Clean Air Act 1956 and, in relation to the City of London, by the City of London (Various Powers) Act 1954.

The Clean Air Act 1956 was introduced to make provision for abating the pollution of the air. Air pollution had, in the 1950s, become a particular problem and many people will still recall the smogs that shrouded London at that time, making living conditions quite intolerable.

Section 1 of the Act, for instance, makes it an offence punishable by a magistrates' court by fine, for the occupier of a building to allow "dark smoke" to be emitted from the chimney.

Section 11 of the Act went further than this and gave the Council power to make smoke control areas, such areas comprising the whole of the district administered by the Council or parts of the district. The orders made by the Council originally needed to be confirmed by the relevant Minister, but since 1980 this is no longer necessary and the Council can make its own orders without submitting them for confirmation.

Before making a smoke control order, the Council must first pass a resolution that it intends to make such an order,

CON 29: PART I STANDARD ENQUIRIES

specifying which part of the district is to be covered by it, if it is not to cover the whole of the district.

The Council then advertises the proposal in the London Gazette and the local newspaper. The advertisement must state the general effects of the order and specify a place where a copy can be inspected during a period of six weeks from the publication of the notice. People who wish to object to the making of the order may do so within this period.

Public notice must also be given of the intention to make a smoke control order. This is done by posting copies of the notice in conspicuous places where persons affected may read the notice.

Any objections received must be considered by the Council. The order may then be made but must not come into force for a period of six months from its being made. When it is made, it must appear in the Register of Local Land Charges and will be revealed in an Official Certificate of Search.

The effect of a smoke control order is that if *any* smoke (not just dark smoke) is emitted from the chimney of any building within the area covered by the order, the occupier of the building may be prosecuted in the magistrates' court for a fine. The only defence to such a prosecution will be that an "authorised fuel" was being used at the time. These "authorised fuels" are smokeless fuels defined in regulations made from time to time by the Secretary of State.

Smoke control orders may make different provisions for different parts of the area which they cover, and may provide for specified classes of buildings to be exempt from the provisions.

Within the approximately one square mile which consists of the City of London (administered by the City of London Corporation) the Corporation promotes private Acts of Parliament from time to time which confer on the Corporation special powers for the administration of what is a very special district. One such private Act was the City of London (Various Powers) Act 1954 which gave the Corporation special powers with regard to smoke control in the City before the Clean Air Act of 1956 was passed.

The City of London (Various Powers) Act 1954 received the Royal Assent and came into operation on 5 July 1954. Within the City it is, by virtue of this Act, a criminal offence to emit

Enquiry 15: Smoke control order

smoke from any premises. The provisions do not apply to smoke emitted from railway locomotives. Offences may be punishable by fines imposed by a magistrates' court, and daily fines may be imposed for continuing offences. "Smoke" includes, for these purposes, soot, ash, grit or gritty particles.

As with the Clean Air Act 1956, the proper use of "authorised fuels" in a properly maintained furnace stove or other suitable appliance will be a defence to any prosecution for breach of the provisions of the Act, and these "authorised fuels" are coke, anthracite or other fuels authorised by order of the Council under s 4(2) of the Act.

An occupier of premises within the City may obtain an order from the court directing the owner of those premises to make a contribution towards the costs of works necessary for complying with the provisions, and the Council may itself make such contributions if it wishes. Such works may include the provision, alteration or adaptation of fixtures, fittings and appliances.

By virtue of s 4(6) and (7) of the Act, the Council may by resolution agree to exempt particular premises from the application of the smoke control provisions, or defer such application to a later date, and a copy of any such resolution must be served on the owner and occupier of the premises to which it relates.

Summary

Enquiry 15 asks whether the property is included within an area for which the Council is proposing to make or vary a smoke control order. If one has already been made, this will be revealed by the Official Certificate of Search since it will be registered as a local land charge. The Enquiry therefore reveals *proposed* orders or proposed alterations to existing orders. Whether a purchaser will prefer a negative or an affirmative response will depend on his individual circumstances. Purchasers of residential properties will generally be quite pleased to have a smoke control order covering their area, since although the types of fuel they may burn will be restricted, so will the types which may be burned by other occupiers. A purchaser of industrial premises will be concerned to know just what the proposals are since they may hamper his operation.

CON 29: PART I STANDARD ENQUIRIES

The purchaser of property within the City of London may be further concerned to know which "authorised fuels" may be burned without risk of prosecution, and whether the property enquired about has been exempted by order of the Council from the smoke control provisions of the 1954 Act.

Enquiry 16: Contaminated land

16.1. *Is the property included in the Register of contaminated land?*
16.2. *If so:*
    (a) *how can copies of the entries be obtained?*
    (b) *where can the Register be inspected?*

This Enquiry concerns entries in the register of contaminated land. Local authorities are required to maintain this register by virtue of s 143 of the Environmental Protection Act 1990.

The Environmental Protection Act is a radical and wide-ranging statute containing new and modified powers and duties for local authorities to deal with a whole host of issues. The Act includes provisions on the following:

- control of industrial pollution
- collection and disposal of waste
- statutory nuisances
- control of offensive trades and businesses
- control of gas emissions
- litter control
- abandoned shopping trolleys
- radioactive substances
- control of genetically modified organisms
- potentially hazardous substances
- oil pollution from ships
- identification and control of dogs
- burning of crop residues

Section 143 of the Act imposes a duty on the local authority, as respects land in its area subject to contamination, to maintain a register in such manner and containing such particulars as will be prescribed by regulations. The local authority charged with this duty is, in Greater London the appropriate London Borough Council or the Common Council of the City of London, and elsewhere in England and Wales, a District Council.

As with many of the powers and duties conferred and imposed by the Act, most of the detailed administrative arrangements have yet to be prescribed by regulations. In particular, it is for the Secretary of State to specify "contaminative uses" of land, which the Act defines as any use of land which may cause it to be contaminated with noxious substances. "Land subject to contamination" means land which is being or has been put to a contaminative use.

The duty imposed on the local authority is to compile and maintain a register of land subject to contamination from information available to the authority from time to time. The local authority is therefore not bound, by this Act, to actively seek out such land.

Summary

Enquiry 16.1 asks whether the property is included in the register of contaminated land. A purchaser will normally raise this Enquiry only in respect of undeveloped land where there is some history of the site having been used in connection with an industrial process or, perhaps, as a landfill site. Naturally, a purchaser will prefer a negative response, but such response will not, of itself, mean that the land is uncontaminated.

If an affirmative response is given to Enquiry 16.1, the prudent purchaser should press for full details of the entries.

* * *

The local authority is obliged to keep the register open to inspection by members of the public, at its principal office, free of charge, at all reasonable hours. The public are entitled to be afforded facilities for obtaining, on payment of the authority's reasonable charges, copies of entries in the register.

Summary

Enquiry 16.2(a) asks how copies of the entries can be

Enquiry 16: Contaminated land

obtained. Since the public is entitled to reasonable facilities for obtaining copies, it is to be expected that copies will normally be despatched to an applicant on payment of the authority's reasonable charges and postage.

Enquiry 16.2(b) asks where the register can be inspected. The register should be maintained at the authority's principal office, normally within the planning department.

Part II Optional Enquiries

The Council will reply only to those Enquiries which the enquirer has indicated by placing a tick in the appropriate panels in Box G on the front of the Form. A charge is made for each individual Enquiry. *Noted by us and details passed to Land charges at end of year.*

Enquiry 17: Railways

What proposals have been notified to the Council, and what proposals of their own have the Council approved, for the construction of a railway (including light railway or monorail) the centre line of which is within 200 metres of the property?

This Enquiry relates to proposals notified to or approved by the Council for the construction of railways, either under special Act of Parliament or by virtue of an order made under the Light Railways Act 1896.

Any person may construct a railway on his/her own land, and no statutory authority is necessary beyond the normal requirement for planning permission in respect of the operational development entailed in its construction. However, since the construction of a railway usually involves the acquisition of land and interference with the private rights of other landowners, a special Act is normally necessary for the purposes of conferring compulsory purchase and other powers on a railway undertaker.

The authorisation and construction of the vast majority of the public railway system in Great Britain are dealt with in the Railways Clauses Consolidation Act 1845 and the Railways Clauses Act 1863. Provisions are made in these enactments for the construction of works, occupation of land in connection with construction, protection of adjacent land, the crossing of roads and construction of bridges, and for the operational requirements of railway undertakers.

Responsibility for the control of the public railway system, and for certain other railway and light railway undertakings, now vests in the British Railways Board and London Regional Transport. A few independent railway undertakings do survive and their functions and powers are contained in their own special Acts.

British Railways and London Transport have power to acquire land for the purposes of their operations, and compulsory purchase powers are available by order of the Secretary of State. Development of operational land (ie land used for the purposes of carrying on the undertaking) by these two bodies has the benefit of permitted development rights under the Town and Country Planning (General Development) Order (see commentary on Enquiry 9). Hence planning permission for development of their operational land is not required. Independent railway undertakers derive authority for acquisition of land and construction works from their special Act.

When a Bill is promoted for the construction of a railway, a plan in duplicate, together with a book of reference and a section of the works proposed, must be deposited with the Council of the county in or through which the railway is to be constructed. An ordnance map showing the proposed line of the railway must also be deposited. Publicity must be given to the proposals and prescribed notices must be served, in particular upon the owners of land required by the undertaker for construction of the railway. Any interested person is entitled to inspect the plans and sections (and any altered plans and sections) and to make copies of them. In constructing the railway the undertaker may deviate from the line shown on the deposited plans within the limits specified for such deviation, but by not more than ten yards from the delineated line when passing through built-up areas, and elsewhere by not more than one hundred yards. In deviating from the delineated line, the undertaker may not extend the railway construction into the land of any person whose name is not mentioned in the book of reference, without that person's consent.

In constructing the railway, the undertaker has extensive powers to build tunnels, embankments, aqueducts, bridges, arches, cuttings and fences, to alter the course of non-navigable rivers, build houses, warehouses, offices and other buildings, yards, stations, wharfs, machinery and such

Enquiry 17: Railways

apparatus as is deemed necessary for the efficient operation of a railway undertaking.

The undertaker may take temporary possession of land (except domestic gardens) within two hundred yards of the centre of the line delineated on the plans for so long as may be necessary for the construction of the railway or associated works. This power to take temporary possession is exercisable without prior payment, but three weeks' written notice must be given to the owners and occupiers of the land (except in the case of accident to the railway requiring immediate repair). During the period of temporary occupation, the undertaker may take earth or soil by side cuttings from the land, may deposit soil on the land, and may take materials for repair or construction of the railway. The undertaker must pay compensation to the occupier of the land within one month of entry, calculated in accordance with the value of any crop or dressing on the land together with full compensation for other damage of a temporary nature. The undertaker must also pay compensation in respect of all permanent loss or damage within six months of completion of the works of construction.

Light railways

Light railways are authorised by order of the Secretary of State for Transport under the provisions contained in the Light Railways Act 1896. Applications for orders may be made by County, District and London Borough Councils, by private promoters (individuals, corporations or companies), or jointly by a Council and a private promoter. Advertisement of the application must be published in a local newspaper for two consecutive weeks and in the London Gazette and notices must be served on persons affected. The line of the railway and its termini, the proposed gauge and motive power of the railway and the land proposed to be taken for construction must be described. A place must be specified in the notice at which plans and sections of the proposed railway and of the land required for construction may be inspected at all reasonable hours, and copies of the draft order must be made available on payment of the specified fee.

The notice and draft order, plans, sections, books of reference, estimate of expenses of the light railway and an ordnance map showing the line of the whole railway must be deposited for inspection by the public with every County,

CON 29: PART II OPTIONAL ENQUIRIES

London Borough, District and Parish Council through whose area the line is proposed to be constructed. Objections and representations may be made in writing to the Secretary of State for Transport (and must be copied to the promoters of the order or their solicitors).

On receiving the application for a light railway order, the Secretary of State for Transport must be satisfied that the local authorities through whose area the railway is intended to pass have been consulted and the owners and occupiers of land proposed to be taken have been notified. A local public inquiry may be conducted into the application and the Secretary of State must be satisfied as to the safety of the public and other material considerations, including the utility of the proposed railway, its advantage to the public, the nature and extent of opposition to the application and the probable effect on existing railways of the competition.

If the Secretary of State agrees to grant an application for a light railway order, he must ensure that all matters necessary for the construction and working of the railway are inserted in the order, including provisions for the safety of the public and particulars of the land proposed to be taken. Provisions of the Railways Clauses Consolidation Acts may be incorporated conferring compulsory purchase powers on the promoters of the railway.

Summary

Enquiry 17 asks for details of proposals notified to the Council, or proposals approved by the Council itself as a railway promoter, for the construction of a railway within 200 metres of the property. A purchaser receiving outline proposals in reply to this Enquiry would be well advised to secure a copy of any plans, sections and relevant extracts from the books of reference which should be on deposit at the offices either of the County (or London Borough) Council or, in the case of light railways, the District (or London Borough) Council. A purchaser of property within 200 yards of the centre line of the proposed railway may be subjected to the rights of temporary occupation by the railway operator during the course of construction. Purchasers of property which is close to the route of a proposed railway line should be aware that during the course of construction the line may deviate, within prescribed limits, from the line shown on the deposited plans.

Enquiry 18: Public paths or byways

Has any public path, bridleway or road used as a public path or byway which abuts on or crosses the property been shown in a definitive map or revised definitive map prepared under Part IV of the National Parks and Access to the Countryside Act 1949 or Part III of the Wildlife and Countryside Act 1981? If so, please mark its approximate route on the attached plan.

This Enquiry relates to public rights of way which may *cross* or *abut on* the property. It will normally only be asked where the property to be purchased consists of open fields or cleared development sites or where a physical inspection of the property has revealed a path which has the appearance of being used by the public.

Public rights of way are rights for the public at large to walk, ride or drive over defined paths or byways crossing land which is otherwise in private ownership. They generally fall into three categories which are defined by the law as follows:

A **footpath** is defined as a highway over which the public has a right of way on foot only, other than a highway at the side of a public road (called a "footway").

A **bridleway** is defined as a highway over which the public has the right of way on foot and a right of way on horseback or leading a horse. There may also be a right to drive other animals along a bridleway.

A **byway open to all traffic** is defined as a highway over which the public has a right of way for vehicles and other traffic but

CON 29: PART II OPTIONAL ENQUIRIES

is used by the public mainly for the purpose for which footpaths and bridleways are used.

The Wildlife and Countryside Act 1981, and in particular Part III thereof, introduced a new code replacing the provisions formerly contained in the National Parks and Access to the Countryside Act 1949 and the Countryside Act 1968, for the preparation and revision of *definitive maps* relating to public rights of way in the countryside. The old provisions were cumbersome and since the revision to the maps would not take effect until all objections and representations had been resolved, decisions took many years to be implemented.

The new definitive map and statement procedure provide for continuous review.

The old classification "road used as a public path" (RUPP) has now vanished. Such roads now have to be classified either as a "byway open to all traffic" (BOAT), a "bridleway" or a "footpath".

It is the responsibility of the surveying authority (generally the County Council or, in London, the London Borough Council) to keep the definitive map showing all public rights of way within its area under review, make modifications to it in the event of such rights of way being stopped up, widened or diverted, upgraded or downgraded (eg bridleway to footpath, BOAT to bridleway), and add such rights of way to the map where new rights are shown to exist.

Any person may apply to the surveying authority for an order making modifications to the map if it can be shown, for example, that a right of way that actually exists is not shown on the map, or that a right of way shown on the map as a right of a particular description ought to be shown as of a different description (eg that a right shown as a footpath should be a bridleway).

There is a formal procedure within the Wildlife and Countryside Act 1981 (Schedule 14) for applying for these orders. In particular an applicant must show documentary evidence, including statements of witnesses, which supports his application. He must also notify the owner of the land to which the application relates. The Council then investigates the application and decides whether or not to make the order. There is a right of appeal to the Secretary of State if the Council refuses to make the order.

Enquiry 18: Public paths or byways

Many of these public rights of way, as defined in the definitive map and statement, are highways maintainable at the public expense (ie by the Council as highway authority on behalf of the community chargepayers) but the Council is not obliged to provide a metalled carriageway and in practice many of the public paths are difficult to negotiate during periods of wet weather. Many public rights of way will be privately maintainable notwithstanding the public right to use them.

Once a right of way appears on the definitive map, it is conclusive evidence of the fact of its existence and the public is entitled to demand its right to pass on foot, on horseback or in motor vehicles, as appropriate to the description of the right of way in question. It will be an offence punishable in the magistrates' court to obstruct the right of the public to pass, even for the owner of the land in question.

A copy of the definitive map and all modification orders must be kept available for public inspection free of charge at all reasonable times in each district to which the map relates (usually at the District Council offices).

There are two other particular restrictions arising by virtue of the existence of a public right of way:

(i) Prohibition on keeping bulls − any occupier of a field crossed by a public right of way, for example a farmer, may not permit a bull to be "at large", ie free to roam in that field, and if he does the occupier may be fined up to £200 in the magistrates' court.

This does not apply if the bull is under the age of ten months or is not a recognised dairy breed and is accompanied by cows or heifers. A recognised dairy breed means Ayrshire, British Friesian, British Holstein, Dairy Shorthorn, Guernsey, Jersey or Kerry.

(ii) Restrictions on ploughing − farmers may be fined for ploughing up rights of way over their land and may be required to reinstate them and restore the surface to a reasonable condition.

Summary

Enquiry 18 asks whether there are any public rights of way over the property *or abutting on it* which are shown in the definitive map or any revision of the map. A purchaser will normally prefer a negative answer since he will not wish to be inhibited in the use to which he puts his land. He will be particularly interested if he intends to farm the land in question, in which case he may need to make special provision for the security of his beasts and crops. It will not be an offence to fence the path off, but it will be to obstruct it, otherwise than by, for example, a stile for pedestrians (provided the right is not a BOAT or bridleway). Developers of cleared sites will also need to ensure that their proposed developments will not obstruct the footpath. The purchaser should always supply a plan with his application for search if he requires a reply to this Enquiry, as the Enquiry asks the Council to mark the approximate route of the right of way on the plan supplied.

Enquiry 19: Permanent road closure

What proposals have the Council approved for permanently stopping up or diverting any of the roads or footpaths referred to in Boxes B and C on page 1?

This Enquiry relates to proposals for the stopping up or diversion of roads or footpaths which are referred to in the description of the property appearing on the front of CON 29. It may well be asked by a purchaser as a corollary to Enquiry 18. The enquirer should take care when requesting a reply to this Enquiry to ensure that any roads or footpaths not mentioned in Box B (description of the property) are adequately described or listed in Box C (other roads etc).

There are a number of statutory powers open to a Council which wishes to stop up or divert a highway (ie a road or a footpath) and these are contained in various Acts of Parliament, depending on the reasons for which the stopping up is sought.

Under s 116 of the Highways Act, the Council may apply to a magistrates' court for an order stopping up or diverting a road on the grounds that it is unnecessary or that it can be diverted so as to make it nearer or "more commodious" to the public. This provision is used at the request of the landowner over whose land the road runs, and indeed it is the only power which can be invoked by a landowner, provided that he can persuade the Council to take action on his behalf.

Notices must first be given by the Council to the owners of all land adjoining the highway, the statutory undertakers concerned, the Parish Council and the Secretary of State in the case of a classified road. A notice must be displayed at each end of the highway to be stopped up and notices must appear in the London Gazette and local newspapers. All these notices must be served or published at least twenty-eight days before the application to the magistrates is made, and any person on whom a notice has been served has the right to be heard by the magistrates before an order is made.

The magistrates may decide to inspect the highway themselves before making the order, and the order, when made, may stop up the highway for all purposes or reserve rights of way for pedestrians, or bridleway rights.

Whilst a landowner may request the Council to make this application on his behalf, if the Council refuses to do so, the landowner cannot apply to the magistrates on his own initiative.

Under **s 118 of the Highways Act**, a special procedure is set up for the stopping up of public footpaths and bridleways. An order extinguishing the public path or bridleway may be made by the Council where the Council considers it expedient that it should be stopped up as it is not needed for public use. If the Council decides to make such an order, notice of intention to make it must first be published and at least twenty-eight days must be given to the public to lodge objections to the extinguishment order. Notices must be served on the owner of the land over which the path passes and be posted at each end of the footpath concerned. If there are no objections to the making of the order, the Council may then make it. If there are objections, the order must be confirmed by the Secretary of State who will only confirm it after he has held a public local inquiry into it to allow objectors to make their representations.

Under **s 119 of the Highways Act,** the Council may make a "public path diversion order" if requested by the owner of the land crossed by a public path. Here the owner of the land will have to show that it is expedient that the path be diverted in the interests of the owner or in the public interest. These diversion orders may be proposed purely in the interests of agricultural management and good husbandry, but the Secretary of State, before confirming the order, must be satisfied on the evidence that the path, when diverted, "will not be substantially less convenient to the public". Otherwise the procedure for making and confirming diversion orders is similar to that for extinguishment orders.

Enquiry 19: Permanent road closure

Section 122 of the Highways Act gives the Council, as highway authority, power to divert a highway temporarily where it is about to repair or widen it. The diversion may be made on to any land adjoining the highway, even without the owner's consent, but the owner will be entitled to compensation for any damage.

Under **s 247 of the Town and Country Planning Act**, an order may be made authorising the stopping up or diversion of a highway where it is necessary to enable development to be carried out under a planning permission which has been granted. Similar provisions in **s 257** of this Act authorise the making of an order stopping up a public footpath where it is necessary to do so to enable development to proceed. In both cases it will be necessary to show to the Council, and to the Secretary of State in the event of objections to the order and a subsequent public local inquiry, that planning permission for the development has been obtained and that it is not possible to carry out the development unless the road or footpath is stopped up. If, by the time the public local inquiry into objections is held, the development has been completed, it is unlikely that the order will be confirmed by the Secretary of State. The developer will then find himself in breach of the Highways Act 1980 for obstruction of a highway by his development and may be prosecuted for this offence or even forced, by injunctive proceedings at the suit of the highway authority, to remove it.

The above is an outline of some of the provisions which may be used to effect a stopping up or diversion of roads or footpaths. It is not exhaustive.

Summary

Enquiry 19 asks whether the Council has considered and approved any proposals for the stopping up or diversion of roads or footpaths referred to in the description of the property. A purchaser wanting a reply to this Enquiry will have to be careful to name or describe all those roads or footpaths enquired about and it would be prudent to attach a plan showing them. The desirable reply will depend on the wishes of the purchaser. A purchaser will not normally want the road fronting on the property to be stopped up or diverted, but he may be quite happy to find that the Council proposes to stop up a footpath crossing the property. Of course an affirmative reply will not necessarily mean that the road or footpath will be stopped up or diverted. It will only mean that the Council has approved proposals to stop up or divert. Most of these orders require the confirmation of the Secretary of State.

Enquiry 20: Traffic schemes

In respect of any of the roads referred to in Boxes B and C on page 1, what proposals have the Council approved, but have not yet put into operation, for:
(a) waiting restrictions,
(b) one way streets,
(c) prohibition of driving,
(d) pedestrianisation, or
(e) vehicle width or weight restrictions?

This Enquiry refers to restrictions on the movement of traffic (or certain classes of traffic including pedestrian traffic) to be imposed by the Council under the Road Traffic Regulation Act 1984 and other legislation.

The duty of the local authority in exercising its functions under the 1984 Act is to secure the expeditious, convenient and safe movement of vehicular traffic and pedestrians and the provision of suitable and adequate parking facilities on and off the highway. The local authority's functions are exercised under the Act largely by way of traffic regulation orders.

Outside Greater London traffic regulation orders may be made by the local highway authority in respect of roads other than trunk roads, and by the Secretary of State for Transport in respect of trunk roads. The highway authority for these purposes is the County Council (or Metropolitan District Council), but in practice in many areas the District Council makes traffic regulation orders on behalf of the relevant County Council under agency arrangements.

The making of a permanent traffic regulation order under section 1 of the Act must be shown to meet one of the following purposes:

(a) avoiding or preventing danger to persons or traffic;
(b) preventing damage to roads or buildings;
(c) facilitating the passage of traffic (including pedestrians);
(d) preventing the use of the road by vehicular traffic which is unsuitable having regard to the character of the road or adjoining property;
(e) preserving the character of a road which is specially suitable for use by persons on horseback or on foot;
(f) preserving or improving the amenities of the area.

Provisions which may be imposed in traffic regulation orders include prohibitions or restrictions regulating the use of a road, or any part of the width of a road, by vehicular traffic of any class specified in the order, and the order may specify exemptions and times of the day or days of the week during which the prohibitions or restrictions will apply.

Examples of restrictions that may be imposed by traffic regulation orders outside Greater London include:

- one-way traffic;
- provision of bus or taxi lanes;
- prohibition of waiting or loading and unloading;
- prohibition of through traffic;
- restrictions on overtaking;
- pedestrian precincts;
- pedestrian bans;
- through routes for or prohibition on heavy commercial vehicles.

The scope of the provisions which may be made by traffic regulation orders is not limited to these examples, but speed restrictions may not be imposed in this way.

A traffic regulation order may not be made so as to prevent access by pedestrians to premises which can only be accessed from the road to which it relates, or to prevent such access by vehicles for more than 8 hours in 24, except in special circumstances.

Once a traffic regulation order has been made, traffic signs must be placed by the authority on or near the road to which

Enquiry 20: Traffic schemes

it relates giving sufficient information of the effect of the order to persons using the road. It is an offence to contravene the provisions of a traffic regulation order but it has been held that if signs conforming to the requirements of the Act have not been duly erected, the order is invalid and contravention will not be punishable by fine or otherwise.

Within Greater London traffic regulation is achieved in respect of non-trunk roads by order of the appropriate London Borough Council, or the Common Council of the City of London, and in respect of trunk roads by the Secretary of State or, with his consent, by the appropriate London Borough Council (or Common Council of the City of London). Orders, which for Greater London are made under s 6 of the Act, may be made for one of the purposes outlined in (a) to (f) above and in addition a further 22 purposes are prescribed in Schedule 1 to the Act. These include, for example:

- prescribed routes to be followed by all or any class of traffic;
- prohibition of U-turns;
- prescribed maximum number, size and weight of trailers;
- conditions upon which horses, cattle and sheep may be driven on streets in London;
- control of broken-down vehicles;
- restriction on use of vehicles, animals and sandwichmen for advertisement purposes;
- lighting and guarding of streetworks.

Orders in respect of Greater London may be made so as to apply to the whole area of the local authority or to particular parts of it, and may apply throughout the day or during particular periods or on special occasions only.

As with orders made outside Greater London, the regulation of speed by orders under s 6 of the Act is not permitted.

Experimental traffic orders may be made both within and outside Greater London for similar purposes and subject to the same restrictions as are outlined above. Experimental orders continue in force for a maximum period of 18 months, but may be continued for a further period of 6 months by the Secretary of State. Experimental schemes may also be introduced for limited purposes, in Greater London, by the

Commissioner of Police. The consent of the appropriate local authority is required for such schemes. These schemes may continue in force for a maximum of 6 months in the first instance, subject to extension by up to a further 6 months with the consent of the local authority.

Temporary orders may be made within and outside Greater London for the purpose of restricting or prohibiting traffic or pedestrians on roads where works are to be carried out, and restriction is necessary to prevent danger to the public or serious damage to the highway. In cases of emergency, similar restrictions and prohibitions may be imposed by the highway authority by notice, if it is necessary that they come into force without delay. Temporary orders and notices may also make provision for temporary speed restriction.

Temporary orders may continue in force for a maximum of 3 months, although they may be extended by consent of the Secretary of State. This limitation does not apply to orders made in Greater London, or by the Secretary of State. Notices imposing temporary restrictions in cases of emergency may not continue in force for more than 14 days.

Special cases

There are further provisions within the 1984 Act in relation to traffic regulations on special roads, one-way traffic on trunk roads, use of highways by public service vehicles, special areas in the countryside (national parks, areas of outstanding natural beauty etc), school crossings, street playgrounds, on and off street parking and general traffic schemes.

Before making a traffic regulation order, the local authority must consult with the police authority and give public notification of its intentions. There are detailed provisions relating to the procedures for making orders and the publicity which must be given to them, and the consideration which must be given to objections and, in the case of permanent orders, there are provisions for the holding of public inquiries into such objections.

Summary

Enquiry 20 asks for details of proposals approved by the Council, but not yet put into operation, in respect of traffic schemes affecting the roads specified by the enquirer; the

Enquiry 20: Traffic schemes

Enquiry relates particularly to waiting, one-way, prohibition of driving, pedestrianisation and weight and width restrictions. Before the detailed procedures contained in the Act are put into effect, the local authority will have considered the proposals and adopted them by formal resolution. A purchaser raising this Enquiry and receiving an outline of the proposals should press for full details of the approved proposals including a date when it is intended to bring the restrictions into force and the full implications of such restrictions. The purchaser will also be concerned to know whether any restrictions are to be of a temporary or permanent nature.

* * *

Pedestrian planning orders

The local planning authority (as opposed to the highways authority) may apply to the Secretary of State for Transport for an order extinguishing the right to use vehicles on a highway, ie a pedestrianisation order. These orders are made with the principal purposes of improving the amenities of an area, and are promoted under powers contained in the Town and Country Planning Act 1990.

Pedestrian planning orders have the effect of excluding vehicular traffic from the roads to which they apply. The emergency services' (fire, police and ambulance) and statutory undertakers' vehicles (water, gas, electricity, telecommunications etc) are excluded from the operation of these orders, and further exclusions may provide for access to premises by, for example, disabled drivers, Post Office vehicles, and service vehicles. The procedure for making pedestrian planning orders provides for public notice of the proposals, consultation with highway authorities, police and statutory undertakers, consideration to be given to objections, and the holding of public inquiries into such objections.

When a pedestrian planning order comes into force, compensation for depreciation in the value of property is due to any person with an interest in land with access to highways to which the order relates. Compensation is calculated in accordance with the principles applicable to compulsory purchase compensation and is payable by the local planning authority.

Once a pedestrian planning order has been made, the authority is invested with powers contained in the Highways Act 1980 to erect structures on the highway to improve its amenity for pedestrians. Seating, lighting, landscaping and small information kiosks are permitted by these provisions to be erected on the pedestrianised highway.

Summary

Enquiry 20(d) specifically asks about proposed pedestrianisation schemes. Although modest pedestrian schemes can be achieved by way of a traffic regulation order, the powers contained within the Town and Country Planning Act are generally used for the more ambitious town centre improvement schemes. A purchaser of property affected by a pedestrianisation scheme will be concerned to know full details of the proposals approved by the Council including the extent of the scheme's operation, and details of any classes of traffic which will be entitled to continue to use the road in question despite pedestrianisation. A purchaser may become entitled to compensation from the local planning authority if the purchase is completed before the order comes into force.

Enquiry 21: Advertisements

Entries in Register
21.1.1. Please list any entries in the Register of applications, directions and decisions relating to consent for the display of advertisements.
21.1.2. If there are any entries, where can that Register be inspected?

Notices, Proceedings and Orders
21.2. Except as shown in the Official Certificate of Search:
    (a) has any notice been given by the Secretary of State or served in respect of a direction or proposed direction restricting deemed consent for any class of advertisement?
    (b) have the Council resolved to serve a notice requiring the display of any advertisement to be discontinued?
    (c) if a discontinuance notice has been served, has it been complied with to the satisfaction of the Council?
    (d) have the Council resolved to serve any other notice or proceedings relating to a contravention of the control of advertisements?
    (e) have the Council resolved to make an order for the special control of advertisements for the area?

This Enquiry relates to the special code of advertisement control contained in the Town and Country Planning

(Control of Advertisements) Regulations and how it may affect the property. It will normally be asked by purchasers of commercial properties who will be concerned to know whether there are any restrictions on the advertisements that may be displayed.

The current regulations are the Town and Country Planning (Control of Advertisements) Regulations 1989.

The Regulations confer powers on the Council, as local planning authority, for the control of the display of advertisements in the interests of *amenity and public safety*.

An "advertisement", for the purposes of the Regulations, means any word, letter, model, sign, placard, board, notice, device or representation whether illuminated or not, in the nature of, and employed wholly or partly for the purposes of advertisement, announcement or direction (excluding memorials and railway signals) and includes hoardings and balloons.

By virtue of Regulation 3, the Regulations apply to the display of all advertisements *except* those ten classes of advertisements specified in Schedule 2 which are broadly as follows:

(a) those displayed on enclosed land and not readily visible from land outside that enclosure;
(b) those displayed within a building and not visible from outside;
(c) those displayed on vehicles or vessels;
(d) those displayed on balloons flown at a height of not more than sixty metres above ground level for a maximum of ten days in a calendar year;
(e) those actually forming the fabric of a building, eg incised stonework lettering;
(f) those displayed on an article for sale or on its container provided they are not illuminated and do not exceed 0.1 square metres in area;
(g) those relating to Parliamentary, European or local government elections up to fourteen days after close of the poll;
(h) those required by Statute;
(i) traffic signs;
(j) national flags flown on a single vertical flagstaff without added inscriptions beyond the approved design of the national flag.

Enquiry 21: Advertisements

Generally, under the Regulations, no advertisement except as above may be displayed without the consent of the Council as local planning authority, and in giving such consent the Council must have regard, in the interests of *amenity*, to the suitability of the use of a site for the display of advertisements having regard to the general characteristics of the locality, including any features of historic, architectural, cultural and similar interest, and, in the interests of *public safety*, to the safety of persons using any roads, railways, waterways, docks, harbours or airfields. In having regard to safety aspects the Council must consider whether any display is likely to obscure or hinder road signs, railway signals or water navigational aids.

Any person displaying an advertisement without the consent of the Council will be liable to prosecution and fine.

Application for consent under the Regulations is made on a form issued by the Council. The application must be accompanied by full particulars of the proposed advertisement and plans and the prescribed fee. The Council must consult with neighbouring local planning authorities which may be affected by the advertisement, the Secretary of State for Transport if the advertisement may affect the safety of users of a trunk road, and other authorities, notably statutory undertakers, giving them fourteen days to make their observations. The Council may then grant the application subject to conditions relating to cleanliness and safety. Advertisement consents generally last for a maximum of five years.

The Council must notify the applicant of its decision within eight weeks of the application. There is a right of appeal to the Secretary of State against refusal of consent or against conditions imposed on the grant of consent.

Once granted, whether by the Council on application or by the Secretary of State on appeal, the consent runs with the land and may be exercised by any owner of the land for the time being (unless it is revoked or modified by the Council) until it expires (ie normally after five years).

The Council, as local planning authority, must keep a register containing details of all applications for advertisement consent including the name and address of the applicant, date of application, details of the advertisement and the decision of the Council (ie grant or refusal) or of the Secretary of State on appeal. The register must be indexed for the assistance of the public inspecting it, and must be kept at the offices of the Council. Entries in the register must be made within fourteen days of the receipt of application.

Summary

Enquiry 21.1.1 asks for a list of any entries relating to the property contained in the statutory register. A purchaser making this Enquiry will be interested to know what, if any, applications have been made and granted or refused, whether those granted are subject to any special conditions, and how long the consents granted are to last.

Enquiry 21.1.2 asks where the register of advertisement consents can be inspected. If the reply to Enquiry 21.1.1 is in the affirmative, the purchaser may wish to inspect the register. It will be kept at the Council's offices, generally in the planning department, and must be kept open to public inspection at all reasonable hours.

* * *

Regulation 6 provides *deemed consent* for the fourteen classes of advertisements specified in Schedule 3 to the Regulations, ie these fourteen classes of advertisements may be displayed *without* express consent, subject to the Council's power to require discontinuance.

These classes are as follows:

- Class 1   functional advertisements of local authorities, statutory undertakers and public transport undertakers (eg "Bus Stop", "To The Library").
- Class 2   miscellaneous advertisements relating to premises on which they are displayed (eg "Dentist", "Solicitor", "Community Centre").
- Class 3   certain advertisements of a temporary nature (eg advertising property or livestock for sale or the carrying on of building works or local cultural events, travelling circuses and fairs).
- Class 4   illuminated advertisements on business premises displayed on the frontage of premises within a retail park and overlooking a communal car park

Enquiry 21: Advertisements

where the advertisement refers to the business carried on and the name and qualifications of the person carrying it on.

Class 5 advertisements on business premises (eg nature of the business carried on or goods or services provided), other than illuminated advertisements.

Class 6 advertisements on the forecourts of business premises (eg as in Class 5 above).

Class 7 flag advertisements (eg on a flagstaff and showing the name or emblem of the person occupying the building).

Class 8 certain advertisements displayed on hoardings (eg hoardings enclosing building sites).

Class 9 advertisements on highway structures designed to accommodate four-sheet panel displays.

Class 10 advertisements for neighbourhood watch schemes.

Class 11 directional advertisements: house building sites (eg advertisements directing potential buyers to a site where residential development is taking place).

Class 12 advertisements displayed inside buildings.

Class 13 advertisements displayed on a site used for the display of advertisements without express consent ever since 1 April 1974.

Class 14 advertisements displayed with express consent after the consent has expired.

The above is only a summary of the fourteen classes. There are detailed requirements for each class and restrictions on the size each class of advertisement may not exceed.

Normally, then, express consent is not required for these fourteen specified classes of advertisement, within the strict limitations detailed in Schedule 3. They have "deemed consent" under the Regulation. However, the Secretary of State may, by direction, order that the provisions of deemed consent be removed from a particular area or in a particular case, so that application for express consent will have to be made to the Council.

117

Before making such a direction, the Secretary of State will publish notice of his intention in the local newspaper and the London Gazette, notify the owner of any land involved and consider objections. If the direction is made, the Council must publish the effect of it in the local newspaper specifying the date the direction comes into force and, thereafter, application for advertisement consent will have to be made before advertisements of any of the fourteen classes specified in the direction can be displayed.

These directions of the Secretary of State are made under **Regulation 7** of the current Regulations and are very similar in effect to directions made under Article 4 of the General Development Order restricting permitted development (see commentary on Part I Enquiry 9: see pages 64–66).

Summary

same as and article 4.

Enquiry 21.2(a) asks whether the Secretary of State is proposing to make a direction under Regulation 7 removing "deemed consent" for any of the Schedule 3 classes of advertisement. If a direction has already been made, it will appear in the Official Certificate of Search. A purchaser will prefer a negative reply since an affirmative reply will mean that he may have to apply for consent for an advertisement for which he could otherwise claim "deemed consent", and the consent of the Council may not be forthcoming.

* * *

Under **Regulation 8** the Council, as local planning authority, may serve a discontinuance notice requiring the discontinuance of the display of an advertisement displayed under the "deemed consent" provisions of Regulation 6 and Schedule 3. The Council may only do this if it is satisfied that substantial *injury to amenity* or *danger to the public* is being caused by the advertisement.

A discontinuance notice is served on the advertiser, owner and occupier of the site, and any other person displaying the advertisement. It must give a specified time (not less than eight weeks) for the advertisement to be removed, and explain the reasons (amenity or public safety) why it is being served. There is a right of appeal against service of a discontinuance notice to the Secretary of State. If the discontinuance notice is

Enquiry 21: Advertisements

not complied with (and if any appeal against its service has been unsuccessful), it will be an offence punishable by fine to continue to display the advertisement.

Summary

Enquiry 21.2(b) asks whether the Council has decided to serve a discontinuance notice. If one has already been served, it will appear in the Official Certificate of Search. A purchaser will prefer a negative reply since an affirmative one will mean that he may be obliged to remove the advertisement complained of.

* * *

As mentioned above, if a discontinuance notice has been served, it will be revealed by the Official Certificate of Search. In these circumstances a purchaser will want to know whether the requirements of the notice have been complied with.

Summary

Enquiry 21.2(c) asks whether any discontinuance notices served on the property have been complied with to the satisfaction of the Council. This part of the Enquiry will only be replied to if the site has already been inspected by the Council's officers. If a special inspection is required to confirm the position, the purchaser may be asked to pay for this. The purchaser will obviously prefer an affirmative reply.

* * *

Section 224 of the Town and Country Planning Act makes it a criminal offence punishable by fine (and a daily fine for a continuing offence following conviction) to display advertisements in contravention of the 1989 Regulations. Furthermore, a person will be deemed to display an advertisement if he is the owner or occupier of the land on which it is displayed or the advertisement gives publicity to his goods, trade or business (unless he can show that the advertisement was displayed without his knowledge or consent). The Council has, under **s 225** of the Act, power to remove or obliterate unauthorised advertisements (placards and posters) but must first give written notice of its intention so to do unless, of course, the placard or poster does not identify the name of the person who displayed it.

Summary

Enquiry 21.2(d) asks whether the Council has resolved to serve any other notices or proceedings relating to control of advertisements. Clearly, a purchaser will prefer a negative reply. If an affirmative reply is forthcoming, the purchaser will require full details of the alleged contravention of advertisement control since, on completion of the purchase, he may find himself in breach of s 224.

* * *

Regulation 18 of the 1989 Regulations provides for the Council to define areas of special control for advertisement purposes. In these areas, only the following advertisements may be displayed:

(a) nine of the ten Schedule 2 classes of advertisement exempted in general from the operation of the Regulations by virtue of Regulation 3 (see above). The exception is balloon advertisements flown at not more than sixty metres above ground level on not more than ten days in a calendar year – these may not be displayed in areas of special control;
(b) thirteen of the fourteen Schedule 3 "deemed consent" classes of advertisement. The exception here is Class 4 – illuminated advertisements on business premises – which may not be displayed in areas of special control;
(c) advertisements with *express consent of the Council* relating to local events, activities, entertainments, for public safety, or for announcement or direction in relation to buildings in the locality.

Areas of special control are made by order of the Council and have to be approved by the Secretary of State. The proposal to make an order defining such an area must be published in the London Gazette and local newspaper, and an opportunity for representations or objections (at least twenty-eight days) must be given. If there are objections, the Secretary of State may, and in certain circumstances must, hold a public local inquiry before confirming the order, with or without modifications.

Enquiry 21: Advertisements

Once the order is made, further press publicity must be given.

In these areas of special control, it will be seen that there are considerable restrictions on the nature of advertisements that may be displayed.

Summary

Enquiry 21.2(e) asks whether the Council has decided to make an order defining an area of special control. If such an order has already been made which affects the property, it will be revealed by the Official Certificate of Search. The purchaser will want to know of proposals to define an area of special control if his business undertaking relies to any extent on the need to advertise. An affirmative reply to this part of the Enquiry may inhibit a commercial purchaser's operation.

Enquiry 22: Completion notices

Which of the planning permissions in force have the Council resolved to terminate by means of a completion notice under s.94 of the T&CP Act 1990?

This Enquiry relates to the duration of planning permissions granted under the Town and Country Planning Act, and the circumstances in which such planning permissions may be brought to an end. It will normally be asked where a purchaser has agreed to buy the property with the benefit of planning permission and it is particularly important to the purchaser that the planning permission can still be implemented.

Once planning permission for a particular development has been granted, be it for development consisting of building operations or for a change of use, the permission granted attaches to the land and may be implemented by whoever is, for the time being, the owner of the land. Land can thus be sold with the benefit of the planning permission which may then be implemented by the purchaser.

However, the Town and Country Planning Act recognises that it is undesirable to have an accumulation of unimplemented planning permissions and encourages early implementation and the bringing of the land into effective use. Whilst there is no rule whereby planning permissions automatically lapse after a given time, the Act does establish a procedure whereby unimplemented planning permissions can be terminated.

Section 91 of the Act provides that, with certain exceptions,

Enquiry 22: Completion notices

every planning permission granted shall be deemed to be granted subject to a condition that the development permitted must be *begun* within five years, or such longer or shorter defined period as the Council, as local planning authority, shall impose. If no period is specified, the five year rule will apply. If development is not begun within the specified period, then the planning permission lapses and any attempt to begin the development after the end of the specified period will be a breach of planning control – ie the development will not be permitted and the Council may serve an enforcement notice on the person purporting to implement the permission which has lapsed.

Section 56 goes on to define what must have been done to show that development has begun within the specified period. If one of the following operations has been carried out on the land within the specified period for commencement of implementation of the planning permission, the permission will not lapse automatically and the developer can at least show that he has complied with the commencement provisions. The operations are:

(i) any work of construction in the course of erection of the building;
(ii) the digging of a trench which is to contain the foundations of the building;
(iii) the laying of underground mains or pipes;
(iv) the laying out or construction of a road;
(v) any change in the use of the land, where that change constitutes a material development.

By carrying out one of the above operations within the specified period (ie normally within five years of the grant of permission) the developer will normally be able to keep the permission "alive". It will be seen that very little need be done to prevent a planning permission lapsing for non-implementation, provided that what is done is genuinely done for the purpose of carrying out the development.

What if development is *begun* within the time limit specified in the planning permission, or the five year period if no other time limit is specified, but the development is not completed? Clearly it would be most unsatisfactory for uncompleted developments to proliferate and for the country to be littered with half-finished building sites. It is for this reason that s 94 of the Act provides a procedure for the termination of planning permissions where development has commenced but has not been *completed*.

Section 94 provides that where the development permitted by the planning permission has been begun within the time limit specified for its commencement, but has not been completed within that time, the Council may serve a *completion notice*, stating that the planning permission will be terminated at the end of a further specified period, which must be at least twelve months after the notice takes effect, so that the owner of the land will have at least one further year to complete the development.

The completion notice is served on the person who is the owner of the land at the time the notice is served. The notice must be confirmed by the Secretary of State and the notice will only take effect after it has been so confirmed. The Secretary of State may extend the period given by the Council for completion of the development, and if the landowner so requests, a public local inquiry into the notice will have to be held so that the owner and the Council may state their case as to why the notice should be confirmed, or alternatively quashed.

If the completion notice is served and is confirmed by the Secretary of State, the planning permission will be invalid except in so far as it authorises any development carried out up to the end of the period specified in the notice for completion of the development. It is therefore a very definite encouragement for the owner of the land to ensure that the development is completed within the time specified in the notice. Any development taking place after the expiry of the time specified in the notice will be carried out without planning permission and the Council may take enforcement action for a breach of planning control.

The Secretary of State may himself serve a completion notice; this has the same effect on a planning permission as if it had been served by the Council as local planning authority. However the Secretary of State must consult the local planning authority before serving such a notice.

Summary

Enquiry 22 asks whether the Council has decided to serve a completion notice under s 94 terminating any of the planning

Enquiry 22: Completion notices

permissions in force in respect of the property. A purchaser will prefer a negative reply, since he will wish to buy the property with the benefit of any existing planning permissions and without the threat of any of them being terminated. If he gets an affirmative reply, he will want to know which planning permission(s) it is proposed to terminate and what period of time he will be allowed under the proposed completion notice to complete the development, before the planning permission will lapse.

Enquiry 23: Parks and countryside

Areas of Outstanding Natural Beauty
23.1. Has any order under s.87 of the National Parks and Access to the Countryside Act 1949 been made?

National Parks
23.2. Is the property within a National Park designated under s.7 of the National Parks and Access to the Countryside Act 1949?

This Enquiry concerns areas of outstanding natural beauty and national parks designated by the Countryside Commission (or, in Wales, the Countryside Council), and which may affect the property. It will normally be asked by a purchaser who is concerned that any of his proposals for development of the property may be hampered by such a designation.

The Countryside Commission was established by the National Parks and Access to the Countryside Act 1949 with the functions of:

(i) encouraging the preservation and enhancement of natural beauty in England and Wales, and particularly in those areas designated as national parks or areas of outstanding natural beauty; and
(ii) encouraging the provision or improvement, for persons resorting to national parks, of facilities for the enjoyment thereof, and for the enjoyment of the opportunities for open-air recreation and the study of nature.

These functions are now performed in Wales by the Countryside Council, established under provisions contained

Enquiry 23: Parks and countryside

in the Environmental Protection Act 1990. References in this commentary to "the Commission" should be taken to include the Countryside Council for Wales.

An area of outstanding natural beauty is *not* a national park. The terms are mutually exclusive. Under s 87 of the National Parks and Access to the Countryside Act, the Commission may make orders designating areas of outstanding natural beauty, if it is felt desirable in the interests of preserving that beauty.

Before making these orders, the Commission must consult all Councils whose area includes any part of the area to which the order is to relate. Then it must publish notice of intention to make the order in the London Gazette and the local newspapers circulating in the areas affected. This gives the public the opportunity to make representations or objections.

The order must then be submitted to and confirmed by the Minister, who must be supplied with copies of all observations made by each affected Council and the public. The Minister may then confirm the order, modify it or refuse to confirm it.

Copies of the order must be kept by each Council whose area includes part of the area designated, and must be available for inspection by the public at all reasonable times.

The Government encourages the Commission in its objectives of conserving natural beauty. It is generally regarded that areas of outstanding natural beauty, when designated, should be used to meet the demand for recreation so far as this is consistent with the conservation of natural beauty and the needs of agriculture. Once an area of outstanding natural beauty is confirmed by the Minister this may be taken as recognition by the Government of the national importance of the natural beauty of the area designated. Councils, as local planning authorities, in preparing their local plans should have regard to the existence of areas of outstanding natural beauty within or covering their area, and will take them into account in making decisions on planning applications.

The Government recognizes that in general it is inappropriate to permit the siting of major industrial and commercial development in areas of outstanding natural beauty and that only "proven national interest and lack of alternative sites" will justify an exception. Applications for planning permission for such major industrial development within areas of outstanding natural beauty are unlikely to be successful.

Over thirty areas of outstanding natural beauty have so far been designated by order covering something over 17,000 sq km in area ranging from the Scilly Isles (16 sq km) and Chichester Harbour (75 sq km) to the Cotswolds (1,507 sq km) and the North Wessex Downs (1,738 sq km), and including such areas as the Quantock Hills, Malvern Hills, Isle of Wight, Chilterns, Sussex Downs, Wye Valley and the Northumberland Coast.

Broadly, the effects of an area being designated as an area of outstanding natural beauty are that:

(i) The Countryside Commission will advise the Council on any development proposed within the area of outstanding natural beauty, if it is consulted by the Council.
(ii) The Council must consult the Countryside Commission when preparing its development plan (structure plan or local plan).
(iii) The Council has power to preserve and enhance the natural beauty of the area.
(iv) The Council may make by-laws regulating land owned by it in the area of outstanding natural beauty.
(v) The range of permitted development under the General Development Order may be restricted.

Summary

Enquiry 23.1 asks whether the property lies within an area of outstanding natural beauty. Whether an affirmative or negative reply is to be preferred by a purchaser will depend on the circumstances of the purchaser and what he wishes to do with the land or buildings he is buying. A purchaser of residential property, for instance, will be happy living in an area of outstanding natural beauty with the protections afforded to the area from adverse planning applications. A developer wishing to establish substantial industrial premises in the area is likely to be disappointed, however, since his planning application for such a development is bound to be questionable. Small industries, however, may be received favourably by the Council as local planning authority. Applications to use, for example, derelict or redundant farm buildings for small industrial concerns may be successful. Any new building within an area of outstanding natural beauty will be expected to be in harmony with the landscape and architecture of the area, and a prospective purchaser must be prepared for this.

* * *

National parks are also designated by the Commission under the provisions of the 1949 Act as part of the Commission's general duty to make provision for the preservation and enhancement of the natural beauty of the countryside, and its use and enjoyment. National parks are extensive tracts of country in England and Wales which, by reason of their natural beauty, and the opportunities they afford for open-air recreation (having regard to their character and position in relation to population centres), are especially worthy of preservation and enhancement.

The Commission's duty in relation to national parks is to determine (and keep under review) those tracts of country appropriate for designation and protection. Before making an order designating a national park, the Commission must consult all relevant local planning authorities affected by the proposed designation. Designation is by way of an order which describes the area by reference to a map and other descriptive statement and notation. Orders made by the Commission have to be confirmed by the Secretary of State. Before submission for confirmation, notice of the effect of the order and the date upon which it was made must be published in the London Gazette and local newspapers. An opportunity must be given for the public to inspect the order and map over a period of at least 28 days. If no objection or representation is lodged, the Secretary of State may confirm a national park order as unopposed, with or without modifications. If objections are lodged, the Secretary of State must convene a public local inquiry and afford objectors the opportunity of being heard by an inspector before a decision is taken to confirm the order. If confirmed, further publicity must be given to the order.

The Commission has a duty to secure that copies of confirmed orders relating to national parks are maintained at its offices and at the offices of each local authority, for inspection by the public at all reasonable times. The Commission may also determine that copies of the order and map be maintained in or near the national park itself.

CON 29: PART II OPTIONAL ENQUIRIES

The principal consequences of an area being designated as a national park may be summarised as follows:

(i) With regard to an area in a national park outside a metropolitan county, the County Council is the local planning authority for all planning functions.

(ii) Administration of the park is through a special national park committee (unless, as is the case in the Lake and Peak Districts, there is a joint planning board).

(iii) There are restrictions on permitted development rights under the General Development Order (see commentary on Enquiry 9).

(iv) The right to undertake certain types of agricultural and forestry development is subject to an obligation to notify (and sometimes to obtain the approval of) the local planning authority.

(v) The Commission may give advice and make recommendations to the local planning authority and Secretary of State on planning issues associated with the national park, and must be consulted by the local planning authority in the preparation of development plans.

(vi) The local planning authority itself has power to take action for the preservation and enhancement of natural beauty within the area.

(vii) The local planning authority may provide accommodation, meals and refreshments, camping sites and parking places, either in a national park or on land in its neighbourhood, and may use compulsory purchase powers to this end.

(viii) A local planning authority whose area includes a national park with a waterway (including one bounded by the sea) may provide public sailing, boating, bathing or fishing facilities, and other forms of recreation. The local planning authority may use compulsory purchase powers to this end.

Between 1950 and 1957 ten national parks were designated under the legislation. These range from the Pembrokeshire coast (583 sq km) and Exmoor (686 sq km) to Snowdonia (2,171 sq km) and the Lake District (2,243 sq km).

Summary

Enquiry 23.2 asks whether the property lies within a national park. Whether an affirmative or negative reply will be

Enquiry 23: Parks and countryside

preferred by a purchaser is again largely a matter of what the purchaser intends to do with the property. There will obviously be considerable attractions for a residential purchaser in view of the limited forms of development which will attract planning permission. Developers intending to establish substantial industrial or commercial premises would not normally choose a national park in which to locate their enterprise. The restrictions on permitted development rights should be further investigated by the intending purchaser of property in a national park. As the County Council will normally be the local planning authority within national parks, enquiry should be made of that authority as to the detailed planning position, except perhaps by the intending purchaser of purely residential property.

Enquiry 24: Pipe lines

Has a map been deposited under s.35 of the Pipe-lines Act 1962, or Schedule 7 of the Gas Act 1986, showing a pipe-line within 100 feet of the property?

This Enquiry is designed to reveal pipe-lines laid or to be laid in close proximity to the property. It is likely to be asked by a purchaser who is aware of the possible presence of such a pipe-line.

1. Pipe-lines Act 1962

A "pipe-line", as defined in the Pipe-lines Act 1962, is a pipe or system of pipes for the conveyance of any thing other than air, water, water vapour or steam. A drain or a sewer is *not* a pipe-line.

The Pipe-lines Act 1962 was passed with the purpose of controlling, in the interests of the public, the construction and diversion of pipe-lines, and to regulate, in the interests of safety, their construction, operation and maintenance.

There are two main types of pipe-line:

(i) "Cross country pipe-line" – where the length is, or will when constructed exceed, ten miles.
(ii) "Local pipe-line" – any other shorter pipe-line.

A **cross country pipe-line** cannot be constructed unless it has construction authorisation issued by the Ministry. It must be constructed along the route marked on the map annexed to such an authorisation. Works for the construction of the pipe-line must generally be commenced within twelve months of the grant of the authorisation.

There are detailed provisions for the procedure to be followed in applying for the authorisation, including the service of notices and plans and the holding of a public local inquiry into objections if there are any.

A **local pipe-line** does not need a construction authorisation but, at least sixteen weeks before works are commenced on its construction, notice of intention to commence works must be given to the Minister with a plan attached showing the route of the pipe-line. Once again, works must then commence on construction of the pipe-line within twelve months of the notice of intention.

Further provisions in the Act controlling the construction of both types of pipe-line cover such matters as:

  (i) diversion of pipe-lines (similar authorisations have to be obtained or notices served);
 (ii) removal of works executed in contravention of an authorisation;
(iii) exceptions for emergency works;
 (iv) provisions for the avoidance of construction of superfluous pipe-lines;
  (v) preservation of amenity;
 (vi) protection of water against pollution;
(vii) obligation to restore agricultural land;
(viii) safety of pipe-lines.

As soon as the construction or diversion authorisation is granted (in the case of a cross country pipe-line), or the notices are served (in the case of a local pipe-line), the person who has been granted the authorisation or has served the notices must deposit with each Council through whose area the pipe-line is to be constructed or diverted a copy of the map annexed to the authorisation or notice showing that part of the pipe-line which is to be constructed or diverted through the area of the Council.

In the case of emergency works for the construction or diversion of a pipe-line, a copy of the plan annexed to an emergency notification to the Minister showing the route of the emergency works must be sent to the Council as soon as possible.

These maps must be deposited under s 35 of the Pipe-lines Act. Failure to deposit them will render the person who fails to deposit them liable to conviction and fine.

The maps must be kept at the Council offices and must be available for public inspection at all reasonable hours free of charge.

2. Gas Act 1986

By virtue of s 58 of the Pipe-lines Act, the general provisions of that Act do not apply to pipe-lines laid for gas supply by a public gas supplier. However, certain of those provisions, namely those relating to the protection of pipe-lines imperilled by buildings, structures or deposits do apply to gas pipe-lines other than those laid in a street, or service pipes, provided a map showing the route of these has been deposited with the Council.

In brief the provisions are that, if the public gas supplier deposits a map with the Council showing the route of the gas pipe-line (this map must also be kept at the Council offices and open to the public at all reasonable hours), then in certain circumstances buildings or structures erected close to the pipe-line may be ordered to be demolished. In particular, if a person so constructs a building that part of it is situated less than ten feet away from the pipe-line route, and the Minister is satisfied that the pipe-line may be damaged as a result, he may, after conducting an inquiry into the matter, order the building to be demolished or order other works to be carried out to the building so as to safeguard the pipe-line.

Similarly, if, without the consent of the Minister, a person deposits earth, refuse or other materials within ten feet of a pipe-line route then, unless the materials were deposited in the course of agriculture or certain street works, the Minister may have the materials removed and recover his expenses from the owner of the land on which they were deposited.

These provisions relating to the protection of pipe-lines relate to all pipe-lines, but they only relate to gas pipe-lines if the map which is required to be deposited under paragraph 5(3) of Schedule 7 to the Gas Act is duly deposited with the Council.

Summary

Enquiry 24 asks whether a pipe-line map has been deposited with the Council (and is therefore open to public inspection) either under s 35 Pipe-lines Act after pipe-line construction or diversion authorisation has been obtained or notices served,

Enquiry 24: Pipe lines

or under Schedule 7 to the Gas Act relating specifically to the pipe-line protection provisions which will thereby apply to a gas pipe-line in the area. The Enquiry specifically asks for information regarding pipe-lines within 100 feet of the property (and this will mean within 100 feet of *any part* of the property). A purchaser will normally prefer a negative reply since he will prefer not to purchase a property so close to a pipe-line. If the property to be purchased is in fact within ten feet of the route of a pipe-line, gas or otherwise, there is the possibility that the property may be the subject of a demolition order if it is subsequently found to adversely affect the condition or safety of the pipe-line.

Enquiry 25: Houses in multiple occupation

Is the property included in a registration of houses scheme (houses in multiple occupation) under s.346 of the Housing Act 1985, containing control provisions as authorised by s.347 of that Act?

This Enquiry relates to houses in multiple occupation and the "control provisions" contained in the Housing Act. It will normally be asked by a purchaser of a house which is already in multiple occupation or has been adapted for such use.

The provisions formerly contained in the Housing Acts 1961 and 1969 are now contained in Part XI of the Housing Act 1985, and particularly ss 346 and 347.

A house in multiple occupation (HMO) is defined as a house which is occupied by persons who do not form a single household, so that the provisions are designed to regulate houses designed or converted into bedsit accommodation, and the aim of the legislation is to ensure that records are kept of all such properties in the interests of limiting the numbers of households occupying them.

Section 346 of the Housing Act provides that the Council, as local housing authority, may make and submit to the Secretary of State for confirmation a registration scheme authorising the compilation of a register for the district comprising houses in multiple occupation.

The Secretary of State may confirm the scheme as submitted or modify it.

Enquiry 25: Houses in multiple occupation

The registration scheme may be for the whole of the Council's district or for part of it. The scheme may specify the particulars to be entered in the register and compel owners of HMOs to notify the Council of any change in those particulars.

The scheme will come into force, once it is confirmed, on a date specified in it, or if there is no such date, one month after confirmation by the Secretary of State. It must be published both before it is made and once it is confirmed, in the local newspaper, giving the public an opportunity to inspect it at all reasonable hours. Once confirmed, the scheme is open to public inspection at the Council offices free of charge and copies must be supplied on request at a charge not exceeding five pence.

Any person contravening the provisions of a registration scheme, for example by failing to notify the Council of changes in the registered particulars, will be guilty of an offence and liable to a prosecution and fine.

Section 347 of the Housing Act now contains the "control provisions". These are provisions which may be contained in a registration scheme for preventing multiple occupation of a house unless:

(i) the house is registered; and
(ii) the number of households or persons occupying it does not exceed the number registered for it.

The "control provisions" *do not apply* where the persons occupying the house form only two households or where, apart from one household, the house is occupied by no more than four persons.

A person contravening the "control provisions" by permitting occupation of the house by more households or persons than the registration permits will be liable on prosecution to a substantial fine for this offence (currently up to £1,000).

Further provisions of the Housing Act enable the Council to extend these "control provisions" so that the Council may refuse to register a house on the grounds that it is unsuitable and incapable of being made suitable for occupation in accordance with the scheme, or that the person having control of the house is not a fit and proper person, or that work needs to be done to make the house suitable for multiple occupation before it may be registered.

CON 29: PART II OPTIONAL ENQUIRIES

If an applicant for registration is refused by the Council, or informed that the house will only be registered after certain works have been carried out, or hears nothing from the Council for at least five weeks after the date of application, he may appeal to the county court who will either confirm, reverse or vary the decision of the Council on the application.

For the purposes of ascertaining whether or not a particular house is registrable under the scheme, or for ascertaining the particulars to be entered in the register, the Council has powers to require any person having an interest in the house, or living in it, to give in writing any information reasonably required by the Council. Failure to give this information, or making misstatements, will render that person liable to conviction and fine in the magistrates' court (currently £100 in respect of failure to give information and £400 in respect of making misstatements).

Summary

Enquiry 25 asks whether the property is included in an area or is a type of house covered by a registration scheme made by the Council and whether such scheme contains the "control provisions". A purchaser of an HMO will want to know whether there is such a registration scheme in existence, since if there is the property may have to be registered under it. He will also want to know whether the "control provisions" are contained in the scheme, since this may affect his prospects of becoming registered in respect of the property. In this case he will almost certainly also want a copy of the scheme, which will be supplied to him by the Council on request if he remits the modest fee prescribed.

Enquiry 26: Noise abatement

Noise Abatement Zone
26.1. Have the Council made, or resolved to make, any noise abatement zone order under s.63 of the Control of Pollution Act 1974 for the area?

Entries in Register
26.2.1. Has any entry been recorded in the Noise Level Register kept pursuant to s.64 of the Control of Pollution Act 1974?
26.2.2. If there is any entry, how can copies be obtained and where can that Register be inspected?

This Enquiry relates to noise abatement zone orders made, or proposed to be made, by the Council. It may be asked by a purchaser who intends to carry out on the property industrial or other operations which may cause above-average noise levels.

Part III of the Control of Pollution Act 1974 contains the code of statutory control of noise nuisance. Councils may serve noise abatement notices on persons responsible for creating noise nuisances or on the owners and occupiers of premises from which the noise is emitted, and these notices may require the abatement of the nuisance. Failure to comply with these notices will amount to an offence punishable by fine. There are particular provisions for the control of noise on construction sites (noisy operations or machinery) and for the control of noise in streets (loudspeakers etc). The noise abatement notice provisions of the Act are soon to become part of the code of statutory nuisance control contained within Part III of the Environmental Protection Act 1990.

Under s 63 of the Control of Pollution Act, the Council may make an order, known as a noise abatement order, designating all or part of its area as a noise abatement zone. The order will specify the classes of premises to which it applies and these classes of premises will be subject to the noise control provisions of the Act once the order is made.

Before making an order, the Council must serve a notice on owners and occupiers of all premises of the class which will be affected and within the area to be covered. Notice must also be published in the London Gazette and the local newspapers. This notice must state the Council's proposals to make the order and its general effect. It must also specify a place (normally the Council offices) where a copy of the order and its map may be inspected free of charge at all reasonable times for at least six weeks. This notice gives those persons to be affected by the order an opportunity to object to it.

If objections are made to the order, the Council must normally consider them, but since these orders no longer require the confirmation of the Secretary of State, they may come into force on a date specified in the order itself, or on such later date as the Council may decide.

Although a Council has a duty to inspect its area from time to time to decide how to exercise its powers concerning noise abatement zones, it has been held that there is no obligation to make such an inspection before making an order and the fact that no inspection has been made will not invalidate a noise abatement order.

Summary

Enquiry 26.1 asks whether the Council has made, *or has decided to make* a noise abatement order designating a noise abatement zone covering the area which includes the property. A purchaser of industrial premises may be concerned if the processes he intends to carry out will be of a noisy nature, and he will therefore normally prefer a negative reply.

* * *

Under s **64** of the Control of Pollution Act, a Council which has designated a noise abatement zone by order in its area must measure the levels of noise emanating from premises

Enquiry 26: Noise abatement

within the zone (provided they are of a class of premises specified in the order) and record all measurements in a register, called the Noise Level Register, which must be maintained by the Council.

A copy of the recordings of measurements taken must be served on the owner and occupier of the premises and that person may, within twenty-eight days, appeal to the Secretary of State against the record. The Secretary of State may issue directions accordingly to the Council, and the Council must comply with these directions.

The Noise Level Register is open to public inspection at the Council offices at all reasonable times free of charge, and copies of the entries must be provided on request and on payment of a reasonable charge.

Once a noise level is registered for particular premises, that level must not be exceeded except with the consent of the Council, and the Council may give this consent subject to conditions as to the amount by which the level of noise may be increased, and the days and hours during which it may be increased. These conditions are recorded in the Noise Level Register.

A person who applies for consent to exceed the registered noise level for his premises, and is refused consent, may appeal to the Secretary of State within three months, and the Council must comply with the decision of the Secretary of State.

It is an offence to allow noise to be emitted from registered premises in excess of the registered noise level and the magistrates' court may impose a fine for this offence. The court may also order the owner of the premises to carry out works to prevent the nuisance recurring, eg to install noise insulation measures.

Where new buildings are to be erected within a class of premises specified in a noise abatement order and within the zone covered by the order, or where a building is being converted into a class of building specified in such an order, the owner or any person who is negotiating to buy the land or building can ask the Council to determine the noise level which will be acceptable as emanating from the premises when constructed or converted. Any noise level so determined will be entered in the Noise Level Register for the premises. Again there are rights of appeal against the Council's decision to the Secretary of State.

CON 29: PART II OPTIONAL ENQUIRIES

The Council may also serve a noise reduction notice in respect of premises to which a noise abatement order applies, if it is considered that the level of noise emanating from those premises is unacceptable, provided that the proposed reduction of noise is achievable at reasonable expense and would result in benefit to the public. These noise reduction notices may have conditions as to times of the day and days of the week during which the noise level is to be reduced. The details of the notice are also entered in the Noise Level Register. The right of appeal against the notice is to the magistrates' court, but it will be an offence punishable by fine not to comply with a noise reduction notice if no appeal is made or if any such appeal has failed.

Summary

Enquiry 26.2.1 asks whether there are any entries in the Noise Level Register relating to the premises. A purchaser will prefer a negative reply, meaning that there is no restriction on the level of noise his operations may cause. If the reply is affirmative the purchaser will want to know details such as the level of noise registered for the premises, details of all measurements taken by the Council, whether any appeals have been made to the Secretary of State and if so the outcome thereof, and whether or not a noise reduction notice has been served in respect of the premises.

Enquiry 26.2.2 asks where the register can be inspected and how copies of entries can be obtained. A purchaser will want to know this, particularly if the reply to Enquiry 26.2.1 is in the affirmative, so that he can inspect the details of all registrations. The register must be kept at the principal office of the Council and will be administered by environmental health officers. The Council must provide facilities for copies of entries to be taken, but is entitled to levy a reasonable charge for this service.

Enquiry 27: Urban development areas

27.1. Is the area an urban development area designated under Part XVI of the Local Government, Planning and Land Act 1980?
27.2. If so, please state the name of the urban development corporation and the address of its principal office.

This Enquiry concerns areas designated as urban development areas, and urban development corporations. It will normally be asked by a purchaser of property within an area of derelict or run down land, mainly within the centres of old towns or where it is known that an urban development corporation has been established.

The Local Government, Planning and Land Act of 1980 provided for the designation of urban development areas and the establishment of urban development corporations to encourage regeneration of these areas. These corporations are set up in metropolitan districts and the inner London boroughs with the purpose of regenerating areas of derelict and run down land, in the national interest.

The areas are designated by the Secretary of State, and the corporations established to provide their regeneration are also established by Parliament.

The corporations consist of a chairman, deputy chairman and up to eleven other members appointed by the Secretary of State (ie they are not elected). They are people who have a special knowledge of the relevant locality.

The objects of an urban development corporation are

principally to secure regeneration of its area and it must do this by bringing derelict land and buildings into effective use, by encouraging the development of new industry and commerce, by measures designed to enhance the environment, and by ensuring that housing and social facilities are available within the area to encourage people to live and work there.

Wide powers are conferred on urban development corporations by the Local Government, Planning and Land Act, and in particular they have power to purchase, manage, reclaim and sell land and buildings, carry out building operations, make arrangements for the provision of water, electricity, gas and sewerage services, carry on businesses for these purposes and do anything else necessary to achieve the primary object of regenerating the area. In addition, these corporations may make financial contributions toward the costs of Councils and statutory undertakers in the discharge of these functions, and may contribute towards the costs of providing certain amenities.

The particular powers and functions of any urban development corporation will be contained in the order of the Secretary of State establishing it. Specific powers vested in the corporations are as follows:

(a) Power to acquire land

The Secretary of State may confiscate land vested in a Council or other public body such as a statutory undertaker and vest it in the corporation by order, subject to the payment of compensation. The corporation may also buy land by agreement or with the use of compulsory powers. Land acquired by an urban development corporation must be either in the urban development area, adjacent to that area and required for the discharge of the corporation's functions in the area, or, whether or not adjacent to the area, required for the provision of services within the area.

(b) Disposal of land

The urban development corporation has a relatively free hand in disposing of its land for securing the overall object of regeneration of the area which it administers. The corporation must, so far as is possible, provide for the reaccommodation of people who were living or carrying on business or

Enquiry 27: Urban development areas

other activities on the land when it was acquired, and who wish to return to the area. Land offered to these people by the corporation must be suitable for their reasonable requirements, although curiously the corporation is not obliged to offer to such a person who was previously carrying on the business of a public house or off licence, suitable alternative accommodation for this purpose.

The corporation, in both disposing of land and developing it, must have regard to the need for preserving features of special architectural and historic interest, and in particular listed buildings.

(c) Planning functions

The urban development corporation may submit to the Secretary of State proposals for the development of any land in its area. The Secretary of State will consult with the Council as the local planning authority for the area and may then approve the proposals. When the proposals are approved, the Secretary of State may make a special development order granting automatic planning permission for any development within the urban development area which is in accordance with the proposals. In this way, the Council, which is normally the local planning authority, may have its responsibilities of considering planning applications taken away. The urban development corporation virtually becomes, in these circumstances, the local planning authority. Indeed, the Secretary of State may actually make the urban development corporation the local planning authority for part or all of its area, giving it the power and duty to receive and consider *all* applications for planning permission for development within the area or that part of the area defined in the order.

These orders of the Secretary of State vesting planning control duties and powers in urban development corporations may also make the corporation responsible for a wide variety of powers otherwise exercised by the Council as local planning authority, and the Council will not be able to exercise the powers in its own area if the order so specifies.

Powers of local planning authorities under the Town and Country Planning Act and Planning (Listed Buildings and Conservation Areas) Act, which may be vested in the urban development corporation, include the following:

- control of listed buildings;
- building preservation notices;
- tree preservation orders;
- control of advertisements;
- enforcement notices;
- stop notices;
- listed building enforcement notices;
- urgent works for preservation of unoccupied listed buildings;
- compulsory purchase of listed buildings in need of repair;
- listed buildings repairs notices;
- conservation area designation.

(d) Other powers

Further powers which may be vested in an urban development corporation may include building control functions, housing authority functions, the granting of rent rebates, the declaration of streets as highways maintainable at the public expense, sewerage functions, public health functions and the granting of loans.

The first urban development corporations to be established were the Merseyside Development Corporation (covering approximately 865 acres of land in Liverpool and the Wirral) and the London Docklands Development Corporation (approximately 5,120 acres in Greater London). Further corporations were established in 1987 at Trafford, the Black Country, Teesside, Tyne and Wear and Cardiff Bay.

The intention is that urban development corporations will be dissolved when their work is done and the area has been regenerated. At this time the assets of the corporation will be transferred to the relevant Councils or statutory undertakers.

Summary

Enquiry 27.1 asks if the property is situated in an urban development area. If the property is so situated, the purchaser will be well advised to make enquiries of the urban development corporation to find out its functions and powers, since it may well be that it is the corporation, and not the Council, which will be the effective local planning authority for the area, and to whom many of the Enquiries on Form CON 29 should be directed.

Enquiry 27: Urban development areas

Enquiry 27.2 asks for the name and principal office address of the urban development corporation to facilitate the purchaser's enquiries into the corporation's powers and responsibilities.

Enquiry 28: Enterprise zones

Is the area an enterprise zone designated under Part XVIII of the Local Government, Planning and Land Act 1980?

This Enquiry concerns enterprise zones established in the area where the property is situated and will normally be asked by a purchaser of industrial or commercial premises or a purchaser of land who wishes to construct or adapt premises for these purposes.

Under the Local Government, Planning and Land Act 1980 (s 179 and Schedule 32), provision was made for selected District Councils (or London Borough Councils) to be invited by the Secretary of State to prepare schemes for areas with a view to them being designated as enterprise zones. Once the scheme is adopted and the zone designated, development for purposes specified in the scheme will be granted automatic planning permission, and certain premises in the zone will be exempted from the liability to pay rates. There will therefore be, in designated enterprise zones, considerable planning control, rating and other advantages for *industrial and commercial* premises. The idea is to encourage in these areas industrial and commercial activity by the removal of tax and rate burdens and by the speeding up of planning and other administrative controls.

The first step is for the Secretary of State to invite the Council to prepare a scheme. The Secretary of State will specify a proposed area and may make directions as to what provisions the scheme shall contain.

Enquiry 28: Enterprise zones

The Council then prepares the scheme, if it wishes (it is not obliged to do so, but if it does, it must contain the provisions as directed by the Secretary of State). The Council must publicise the scheme it has prepared, and give an opportunity for representations to be made to the Council about it within a specified period of time. The Council must then consider any representations made.

Once the representations have been made, the Council may formally adopt the scheme, with or without modifications, and give public notification of its adoption in the London Gazette and local newspapers, placing a copy of it on deposit at the offices of the Council for public inspection. The public may request copies of the scheme which must be provided at reasonable cost. The importance of the opportunity to inspect the scheme lies in the fact that it will reveal the forms of development that will automatically be granted planning permission in the event that the area later becomes designated as an enterprise zone.

Any person who is aggrieved by the provisions of the scheme adopted by the Council may question its validity within six weeks of its publication in the press by making application to the High Court.

The final step is designation of the enterprise zone. This is done by the Secretary of State, if he thinks it expedient to do so, once the six-week period referred to above has passed or, if an application to question the scheme's validity has been made to the High Court, once those proceedings have been dealt with.

The Secretary of State designates the enterprise zone by order which specifies:

  (i) the date the designation takes effect;
  (ii) the period it is to remain in force (normally ten years);
  (iii) the boundaries of the zone (by reference to a map);
  (iv) the enterprise zone authority (the Council which was invited to prepare the scheme).

Further publicity must then be given about the designation, and an advertisement must be placed in the London Gazette and local newspaper containing a statement that the enterprise zone has been created and that a copy of the scheme from which it was created can be inspected at the Council's offices.

CON 29: PART II OPTIONAL ENQUIRIES

The Secretary of State may modify enterprise zones but *not* so as to alter boundaries, change the enterprise zone authority or reduce the period during which the zone is to be an enterprise zone.

Over seventy enterprise zones have to date been designated in areas such as Swansea, Salford, Trafford, Gateshead, Newcastle, Hartlepool, Liverpool, Isle of Dogs, Wellingborough, North West Kent, North East Lancashire and Telford.

There are particular consequences of an area being designated as an enterprise zone which may be of advantage to the purchaser of *commercial or industrial* property or a purchaser who wishes to establish commercial or industrial undertakings in the zone. These are outlined below:

(a) Planning and development control

One of the main reasons for designating an area as an enterprise zone is to encourage and attract the growth of industrial and commercial undertakings in the area, and for this reason it is desirable that planning permission for such development should be more easily obtainable in such zones. The order designating the zone has the effect of granting *automatic planning permission* for any class of development specified in the scheme. These automatic planning permissions will only be subject to the conditions specified in the enterprise zone scheme, and if none are specified, the permission for that class of development will be unconditional. The scheme therefore provides a form of permitted development rights, and the enterprise zone authority may, with the approval of the Secretary of State, withdraw these rights by direction. Development authorised under an automatic planning permission provided by the order designating an enterprise zone will no longer be permitted once the zone terminates (ie normally ten years from its designation), and application for formal permission to implement that development thereafter will have to be made to the Council as local planning authority, unless the development had commenced before the enterprise zone terminates.

(b) *Rates*

Exemption from the liability to pay rates (but not water rates or charges) is granted in respect of any premises exempted under the scheme for an enterprise zone for so long as the zone remains so designated. All premises in an enterprise zone qualify for this exemption except private dwellinghouses (in respect of which rates have now been abolished and substituted by the community charge), garages and storage premises, and certain premises owned by public utility companies. Partial exemption is granted where the premises are partly private residential and partly otherwise occupied. The loss of rates caused by this exemption to the Council as rating authority is compensated for by government grant.

(c) Other advantages

Apart from the streamlining of the planning process and the rate exemption benefits accruing to industrial and commercial premises within enterprise zones, there are further advantages to owners of such premises in such zones, such as substantial tax advantages and the exemption from the requirement to pay industrial training levies under the Employment and Training Act 1981.

Summary

Enquiry 28 asks whether the property lies within an enterprise zone. A purchaser of commercial or industrial property or one who wishes to establish such an undertaking will be pleased with an affirmative reply in view of the substantial planning, rating and tax advantages available to him. Such a purchaser would however be wise to request a copy of the scheme on which the designation was based for full details of permitted development and the conditions that may be imposed on such a development by the automatic planning permission provisions of the scheme.

Enquiry 29: Inner urban improvement areas

Have the Council resolved to define the area as an improvement area under s.4 of the Inner Urban Areas Act 1978?

This Enquiry is concerned with improvement areas declared in inner urban areas under provisions contained in the Inner Urban Areas Act 1978. It will normally be asked by the purchaser of industrial or commercial property or a purchaser who wishes to establish such a concern within an inner urban area.

The Inner Urban Areas Act introduced measures intended to deal with inner city decay. It attempts to do this by attracting new development to these areas by the offer of grants and loans to facilitate such development.

Districts may be designated under the Act by the Secretary of State if it is considered that "special social need" exists within an "inner urban area" within that district, and that conditions could be alleviated by use of the powers in the Act. The Secretary of State may designate by order the whole or any part of the district concerned and the Council for the district or county becomes the "designated district authority".

Once designated, the Council, as designated district authority, may make loans to persons to enable them to acquire land or carry out works if such acquisition or works would benefit the designated district. Loans of up to 90% of the value of the property to be purchased or of the value of that property after the works have been carried out may be made

Enquiry 29: Inner urban improvement areas

and these loans are secured by mortgages at rates of interest fixed by the Treasury, repayable over a maximum of thirty years.

A number of districts have been designated under this Act. They include, for example, Barnsley, Burnley, Doncaster, Ealing, Greenwich, Hartlepool, Lewisham, Rotherham, Walsall and Wigan.

The designated district authority for each of these areas designated by the Secretary of State (ie generally the District or County Council for the area concerned) may declare improvement areas under s 4 of the Act.

This they may do if they are satisfied that conditions within that area (which is predominantly industrial or commercial in nature) could be improved by the exercise of their powers to make grants and loans.

The Council, as designated district authority, must first pass a *resolution* declaring the area to be an improvement area, specifying a date on which the declaration is to take effect (at least three months after the date of the resolution). The Council must then publish in the local newspaper notice of the effect of the resolution identifying the area to be declared an improvement area, and specifying a place where a copy of the resolution and a map defining the area concerned can be inspected at all reasonable times. A copy of the resolution and the map must also be sent to the Secretary of State.

Termination of improvement areas (whether all of the area or part of it) is dealt with in a similar way, ie by resolution of the Council, publicity of the resolution and map, and despatch of copy of the resolution and map to the Secretary of State.

Within areas declared by designated district authorities (ie Councils) as improvement areas under s 4, the Council may, if satisfied that the carrying out of certain works on land would benefit the area, make loans and grants for enabling those works to be carried out. The works for which these loans or grants may be made are as follows:

   (i) construction of fencing and walls;
  (ii) landscaping and the planting of trees, shrubs and plants;
 (iii) clearance or levelling of land;
 (iv) cleansing, painting, repair or demolition of structures or buildings; and

(v) construction of parking spaces, access roads, turning heads or loading bays.

The Council may also make grants to people to enable them to carry out in improvement areas the conversion, extension, improvement or modification of industrial or commercial buildings, and the conversion of other buildings into industrial or commercial buildings. These grants will not exceed 50% of the cost of carrying out the works and the authority must be satisfied that the works would benefit the areas concerned.

Summary

Enquiry 29 asks whether the property is situated in an improvement area which the Council has *resolved to define* under s 4 of the Inner Urban Areas Act. A purchaser of commercial or industrial premises or of land which it is intended to be developed for these purposes will normally prefer an affirmative reply since he may qualify for the loans and grants outlined above.

Enquiry 30: Simplified planning zones

30.1. Is the area a simplified planning zone adopted or approved pursuant to s.83 of the T&CP Act 1990?
30.2. Have the Council approved any proposal for designating the area as a simplified planning zone?

This Enquiry relates to simplified planning zone schemes proposed or adopted by the local planning authority or approved by the Secretary of State since their introduction to the regime of planning control in 1987.

The adoption (or approval by the Secretary of State) of a simplified planning zone has the effect of granting, in relation to the zone (or any particular part of it), planning permission for the classes of development specified in the scheme. Thus simplified planning zone schemes operate to confer a form of permitted development rights in respect of property to which they relate. Development of land, within the confines specified in the scheme, will not require individual planning permission; this is automatically granted by the scheme subject to any specified conditions or limitations.

The provisions relating to simplified planning zones were first brought into force on 2 November 1987, and are now contained in sections 82 to 87 of the Town and Country Planning Act 1990. There is generally no obligation upon a local planning authority to promote a simplified planning zone. The duty of the local planning authority is to consider, as soon as practicable after the provisions came into force, whether or not such a scheme is desirable for its area (or part of its area), and to keep this question under review. If such a scheme is considered desirable, the local planning authority is under a duty to prepare one.

However, any person has a right to ask the local planning authority to make or alter a scheme. If the authority refuses such a request, the Secretary of State may be asked to intervene. If the Secretary of State, after consultation, is satisfied that a scheme should be made or altered, he may so direct the local planning authority.

The procedures for introduction of a simplified planning zone scheme are very similar to the local plan procedures. An outline of the procedure is as follows:

(i) The local planning authority decides to make a scheme (or is directed by the Secretary of State so to do). The Secretary of State must be notified of the local planning authority's decision and the date upon which preparation will begin.

(ii) The local planning authority must give publicity to the proposals and give adequate time for representations to be made and considered. Consultation with the highways authorities must follow.

(iii) The draft scheme must be placed on deposit for public inspection, and give sufficient time for objections to be lodged. A copy of the draft scheme must be forwarded to the Secretary of State. Objections must be made in writing within 6 weeks of the date upon which the proposals are first available for inspection.

(iv) An inquiry must be held into any objections made within the statutory time limit (6 weeks). The inquiry inspector reports to the local planning authority rather than to the Secretary of State.

(v) The local planning authority must consider any objections made and the inspector's report, and make decisions and recommendations for action in the light of the report, giving a statement of its reasons for any action proposed. The proposals, as originally prepared or as modified to take account of objections, may then be formally adopted by the local planning authority. The Secretary of State may direct the local planning authority to consider further modifying the proposals and there is power for the Secretary of State to call them in for his own approval at any time before they are adopted by the authority.

Enquiry 30: Simplified planning zones

(vi) Adoption (by the local planning authority) or approval (by the Secretary of State) has the effect of granting planning permission in accordance with the scheme in respect of land covered by it, from the date of adoption or approval and for a period of 10 years thereafter.
(vii) A simplified planning zone scheme may be altered at any time (subject to the approval of the Secretary of State if the original scheme was subject to such approval). The procedures for alteration are similar, but may be streamlined where the proposed alterations are not sufficient to warrant the complete procedure being invoked.

Contents of a simplified planning zone scheme

A scheme must consist of:

- a map;
- a written statement;
- diagrams, illustrations and descriptive matter, as appropriate;

and must specify:

- the development or classes of development permitted by the scheme;
- the land in relation to which permission is granted;
- any conditions, limitations or exceptions subject to which permission is granted.

A scheme may specify conditions or limitations in respect of particular descriptions of development, much as an ordinary planning permission granted by the local planning authority on application will, more often than not, be conditional. However, a simplified planning zone scheme cannot affect the right of any person to do anything which does not itself amount to development (as defined in the Act) or to carry out development for which planning permission is not required (permitted development) or for which planning permission has been granted. Conditions imposed in a simplified planning zone scheme are enforceable by the local planning authority in the same manner as those imposed on the normal grant of planning permission (ie by service of enforcement notice – see Enquiry 8).

Simplified planning zones cease to have effect 10 years after the date of adoption or approval, and planning permission under such a scheme ceases to have effect at that time, except in so far as development authorised by it has been begun.

Certain classes of land may not be included in a simplified planning zone. These are:

- land in a national park;
- land in a conservation area;
- land within the Broads;
- areas of outstanding natural beauty;
- Green Belt land;
- areas of special scientific interest.

Summary

Enquiry 30.1 asks whether the area including the property enquired about is a simplified planning zone either adopted (by the local planning authority) or approved (by the Secretary of State). If a negative response is given, the general regime of planning control will apply in the absence of any contrary indication elsewhere in the replies (for instance, a reply to the effect that the property lies within a conservation area or enterprise zone). If an affirmative response is forthcoming, the prudent purchaser will be well advised to press for full details of what is comprised in the scheme since it may affect future intended development of the property and facilitate those intentions by means of automatic planning permission. The purchaser may also be concerned by the possible uses to which premises in the immediate vicinity may be put, without the requirement of formal application for and grant of planning permission. The purchaser will wish to know the date of adoption (or approval) and the expiry date of the scheme.

Enquiry 30.2 asks whether the Council has considered and approved proposals for designating a simplified planning zone. This part of the Enquiry will be relevant where the Council has decided to introduce a scheme but the scheme has not yet reached the stage where it has gone through all the preparation, publicity, consultation and inquiry processes leading up to formal adoption or approval. Depending on his future intentions for the property, the prudent purchaser who obtains an affirmative response to this part of the Enquiry is well advised to press for full details of the approved proposals.

Enquiry 31: Land maintenance notices

Have the Council authorised the service of a maintenance notice under s.215 of the T&CP Act 1990?

This Enquiry concerns the Council's powers to secure the proper maintenance of land within its area by the service of a land maintenance notice under the Town and Country Planning Act 1990. The relevant provisions are contained within sections 215 to 219 of that Act.

The Council, as local planning authority, is empowered by these provisions to take action, principally in respect of neglected wasteland which has become derelict or unsightly to such an extent that the amenity of the area (or the amenity of an adjoining area) is adversely affected. The power now extends to any land within the authority's area and is not, as previously was the case, limited to vacant sites or open land. This provision is a rare example of planning control directed at acts of omission, rather than commission.

If the local planning authority is satisfied that the amenity of part of the area is "adversely affected" by the condition of a particular piece of land, it may serve a notice under section 215 of the 1990 Act on the owner *and* occupier of the land in question. Any such notice will require steps to be taken to remedy the condition of the land within a time specified in the notice. The notice takes effect, subject to any appeal, on the date specified for this purpose in the notice (which must be at least 28 days after service). Failure to comply with the requirements of a land maintenance notice within the time specified in it for compliance will render the owner or occupier of the land liable to summary prosecution and fine. It will be a defence to such prosecution to prove that failure to comply was attributable to the default of another person specified in the original notice and that the defendant took all reasonable steps to ensure compliance in the circumstances.

Conviction of the offence of non-compliance with the notice does not itself relieve the defendant from the obligation to comply with its requirements, and if all necessary steps are not taken the offender may be liable to a daily penalty for so long as the requirements of the notice remain unfulfilled.

There are provisions, contained within section 217 of the Act, for appeal against a land maintenance notice. Any person on whom such a notice has been served, or any other person with an interest in the land to which it relates, may appeal to a magistrates' court on any of the following grounds:

(a) the condition of the land does not adversely affect the amenity of the area;
(b) the condition of the land is attributable to and arises out of the carrying out of operations which have the benefit of planning permission;
(c) the requirements of the notice are excessive;
(d) the period allowed for compliance with the notice is insufficient.

Any appeal must be lodged before the date specified in the notice upon which it is to become effective. If an appeal is lodged, the effectiveness of the notice is suspended pending final determination of the appeal, or its withdrawal. In determining an appeal the magistrates may quash the notice, uphold it or vary its terms in favour of the appellant (but not in favour of the local planning authority).

Either the appellant or the local planning authority may further appeal the matter to the Crown Court.

In default of compliance with the notice the Council, as local planning authority, has further direct powers (in s 219 of the Act) to take the required action itself. The Council may enter the land to take such remedial action, and may recover from the owner of the land for the time being any expenses reasonably incurred. Any expenses are recoverable from the owner or occupier as a simple contract debt.

Land maintenance notices served under s 215 of the 1990 Act are registrable in the Register of Local Land Charges and

Enquiry 31: Land maintenance notices

should be revealed by an official search of the Register. Until drafted, prepared and served the notice has no legal effect and as such will not be registered. The decision to serve such a notice will normally be taken by the Council, or its planning committee, after consideration of a report made by its officers. It is this, as yet, unexecuted decision of the Council to serve a land maintenance notice, that this Enquiry is designed to reveal.

Summary

Enquiry 31 asks whether the Council has authorised the service of a land maintenance notice under s 215 of the Town and Country Planning Act. A purchaser will prefer a negative answer. If an affirmative response is given, the purchaser ought, at the very least, to require full details of the circumstances giving rise to the decision to serve the notice. If the purchaser proceeds with the transaction, he will be obliged to comply or secure compliance with the notice, or appeal against its provisions, and potentially meet any consequential costs of compliance.

Enquiry 32: Mineral consultation areas

Is the area a mineral consultation area notified by the county planning authority under Sched.1 para 7 of the T&CP Act 1990?

This Enquiry concerns the processing of planning applications by district planning authorities in those areas notified by county planning authorities as mineral consultation areas. The Enquiry is not relevant where the property enquired about is within a metropolitan county or London borough.

The general system of planning policy and control under the Town and Country Planning Acts provided for preparation of structure plans by County Councils and of local plans by District Councils. Preparation of these plans is further considered in the commentary on Enquiry 1. The day-to-day functions of the local planning authority in considering and determining applications for planning permission and in enforcing the regime of planning control by enforcement notice and prosecution are generally carried out by District Councils acting as the district planning authority.

Schedule 1 to the Town and Country Planning Act 1990 defines "county matters". These are specific matters in respect of which the local planning authority's functions of determining applications for planning permission are to be exercised by the county planning authority. Most of these "county matters", where the County Council assumes the functions of the district planning authority, relate to the winning and working of minerals or the disposal of mineral waste. Some of the more important defined county matters are:

(i) the winning and working of minerals in, on or under land, or the erection of buildings, plant and machinery to be used in connection with such an operation;
 (ii) the use of land, adjoining land used for the winning and working of minerals, in connection with the adaptation for sale of the minerals;
(iii) the carrying out of searches for and tests of mineral deposits;
(iv) the disposal of mineral waste;
 (v) the use of land for transport by rail or water of aggregates (ie sand and gravel, crushed rock, artificial materials of similar appearance);
(vi) the erection of buildings, plant or machinery to be used for the coating of roadstone or production of concrete, on land adjoining land used for the winning and working of minerals;
(vii) the erection of buildings etc to be used for the manufacture of cement.

Although all applications for planning permission are still to be made to the district planning authority (ie generally the District Council), that authority must send a copy of any planning application, relating to a county matter, to the county planning authority, within 7 days of receipt. It will then be for the county planning authority (County Council) to determine the application.

Paragraph 7 of Schedule 1 to the 1990 Act provides that local planning authorities in non-metropolitan counties must, when determining planning applications and carrying out statutory consultation procedures, seek the achievement of the overall objectives of any structure plan which is in force in the area. This provision is aimed at securing a consistency of approach between district and county planning authorities where the planning function is split between them.

In the interests of bolstering this consistency of approach and co-operation between the two tiers of planning authority which exist (except in London and the metropolitan counties), there is a statutory obligation placed upon district planning authorities to consult their county planning authority colleagues before determining applications for specified types of development.

Of first importance is the duty of the district planning authority to consult the county planning authority before

CON 29: PART II OPTIONAL ENQUIRIES

determining any application for planning permission for development which would conflict with or predjudice policies or proposals contained in a structure plan by virtue of its scale, nature or effect.

In view of their status as county matters, the county planning authority may notify the district planning authority of any area in which development is considered to be likely to be affected by the winning and working of minerals, other than coal. If such notification has been given in writing, the district planning authority is obliged, by virtue of paragraph 7(2)(c) of Schedule 1 to the 1990 Act, to consult the county planning authority before determining any application for development of land within that area (unless the county planning authority has issued directions authorising such determination without consultation). It is with these so-called "mineral consultation areas" that this Enquiry is concerned.

Summary

Enquiry 32 asks whether the area in which the property is situated has been notified to the district planning authority as one in respect of which applications for planning permission require consultation with the county planning authority in view of their implications for mineral extraction operations. A purchaser will normally require a response to this Enquiry only if the intention is to use the property in connection with such an operation or if such operations are already being undertaken on or in close proximity to it. Consultation with the county planning authority may give rise to delay in the process of a planning application. Close proximity to mineral workings may affect the outcome of an application for planning permission, and special conditions may be attached to the grant.

Enquiry 33: Hazardous substance consents

33.1. *Please list any entries in the Register kept pursuant to s.28 of the Planning (Hazardous Substances) Act 1990.*
33.2. *If there are any entries:*
    (a) how can copies of the entries be obtained?
    (b) where can the Register be inspected?

This Enquiry concerns the public register of applications, consents, revocations, modifications and directions issued or made in accordance with the Planning (Hazardous Substances) Act 1990.

The Act brings into force an outline regime of control in respect of defined "hazardous substances", in excess of the "controlled quantity", kept on, over or under land. It is the *presence* of a hazardous substance on (or over or under) land which requires the consent of the hazardous substances authority, not the use of the land or any buildings on it *per se*. This is an extension of the duties of traditional local planning authorities. Although the regime of hazardous substance control is similar in many ways to the regime of planning control, the emphasis which has been placed upon the presence and nature of the substance, as opposed to the use of the land on which it is present, is recognised by the fact that provisions originally contained within the Town and Country Planning Acts have been extracted and consolidated in the new Act. Detailed control provisions will be contained in regulations to be made by the Secretary of State.

The **hazardous substances authority** for the area to which application for consent is made is, in most cases, the local planning authority. In Greater London the authority is the relevant London Borough Council. Outside London, the District Council (or Metropolitan District Council in a metropolitan area) has this duty; in urban development areas (see Enquiry 27) it is generally a function of the urban development corporation. In respect of national parks, the hazardous substances authority is the County Council – there are separate arrangements relating to the Norfolk and Suffolk Broads (the Broads Authority) and operational land of statutory undertakers ("the appropriate Minister").

"Hazardous substances" and their respective "controlled quantities" are to be defined in regulations to be made by the Secretary of State. The Secretary of State may also prescribe, by regulation, descriptions of land and other circumstances in respect of which hazardous substances consent will not be required.

Consent for hazardous substances (referred to in the Act as "**hazardous substances consent**") is not required if the aggregate quantity of the substance on the land (including other land or structures within 500 metres and controlled by the same person) is less than the prescribed controlled quantity for that substance. The temporary presence of a hazardous substance in transit is not taken into account unless it is unloaded.

Hazardous substances consent may either be granted on application to the relevant authority or, in certain limited circumstances, may be deemed to have been given. An applicant need not have an interest in the land to be the subject of the consent, but the owner of the land is required to be notified of any application. Once granted, the consent runs with the land in question and for the benefit of all persons interested in the land from time to time, subject to revocation (see below).

Detailed provisions relating to the form and manner in which applications for consent are to be made, particulars which such applications must contain, consultation to be conducted and publicity to be given to applications, and the time within which they must be dealt with, will be the subject of regulations to be made by the Secretary of State. The Act itself provides only the regime of control. Much of the detailed administrative arrangements has yet to be introduced.

The hazardous substances authority to whom application for consent is made may grant consent unconditionally, or subject to conditions, or may refuse such consent. In reaching its decision on the application, the authority is required to have regard to other land uses in the area and any planning permission granted for other land in the vicinity. Regard must also be had to any advice given by the Health and Safety Executive or Commission following consultation. Application for hazardous substances consent will often go hand in hand with an application for planning permission in respect of the same land. However, the presence of hazardous substances on land will not always require planning permission (eg use of existing storage facilities) so that the only controls available to the authority may be those conferred by this Act.

Conditions may be imposed on the grant of hazardous substances consent relating to the site itself and to each substance it is sought to introduce to the site including, for example, the times between which each substance may be present. There is, perhaps surprisingly, no requirement in the Act relating to qualifications or experience of the person having control of any site the subject of hazardous substances consent.

Application may be made to remove conditions from a hazardous substances consent. On such application, the hazardous substances authority is entitled only to review the conditions attached to the consent. The authority is not entitled to review the question of whether consent should or should not have been granted in the first place.

1. Deemed consent

(a) Established uses

As a transitional measure, deemed consent applies in relation to the established presence of a hazardous substance on land if it has existed for at least 12 months before the date upon which the Act came into force and is claimed within 6 months after that date. If a claim for such deemed consent is made, and not rejected as invalid within two weeks of the claim, deemed consent applies.

(b) Government authorisation

A government department may direct that hazardous substances consent is deemed to have been granted in respect of a development to be carried out by a local authority or statutory undertaker (railway, road transport, water transport operators, gas suppliers, sewerage undertakers etc).

2. Revocation of consent

Hazardous substances consent may by order of the authority be revoked or modified, subject in some cases to confirmation by the Secretary of State. In certain cases the hazardous substances authority will be liable to pay compensation to the landowner, or others affected by a revocation order, for depreciation in the value of the interest in the land or for disturbance. The circumstances giving rise to the revocation of consent are, in brief, as follows:

(a) generally, where the authority considers it expedient, having regard to a "material consideration" (compensation payable);
(b) where there has been a material change of use of the land to which the consent relates (no compensation payable);
(c) where the substance or substances have not been present in a controlled quantity for at least 5 years (no compensation payable);
(d) where there has been a change of person in control of part (as opposed to the whole) of the land – this gives rise to automatic revocation unless an application for continuance of the consent has already been made (no compensation payable except where an application for continuance has been made and the consent is modified or revoked);
(e) where a contravention notice (see below) has been served requiring removal of the substance from the land (no compensation payable if the requirements of the contravention notice are upheld on appeal).

Appeal may be made to the Secretary of State against refusal by the authority to grant hazardous substances consent, or against conditions imposed by the authority on such a consent. Appeal can also be brought where an application for continuation of a consent on a change of person in control of the land is refused or granted subject to conditions unacceptable to the person in control.

Enquiry 33: Hazardous substance consents

The following criminal offences are created by the Planning (Hazardous Substances) Act 1990:

- equalling or exceeding the controlled quantity of a hazardous substance where there is no hazardous substances consent;
- exceeding the maximum quantity permitted by a hazardous substances consent;
- failure to comply with a condition attached to a hazardous substances consent.

Hazardous substance contravention notices may be served by the authority as a method of enforcing compliance with the control provisions of the Act. These notices may be served independently of, or in addition to, the remedy of criminal prosecution. They have a parallel in the enforcement notice provisions and procedures contained in the Town and Country Planning Act (see Enquiry 8 above), although there is no procedure equivalent to the service of a stop notice.

Contravention notices must specify the alleged breach of control and specify steps to be taken to remedy the contravention. They are served on the owner of the land to which they relate, and any other person in control of the land. A reasonable period of time (not less than 28 days) must be allowed for compliance. Provision has been made for an appeals procedure, with right of appeal to the Secretary of State; the effectiveness of the contravention notice is suspended pending final determination or withdrawal of any appeal.

Hazardous substances authorities must, by virtue of s 28 of the Act, maintain a **register** available for inspection by the public at all reasonable hours. The register must record details of all applications, consents, revocations, modifications and directions issued. Each consent granted by the authority must contain:

- a description of the land to which the consent relates;
- a description of the hazardous substance(s) to which it relates;
- a statement of the maximum quantity of each substance permitted by the consent to be present at any one time.

Summary

Enquiry 33.1 asks for a list of entries in the register of hazardous substances. The residential purchaser will not normally be concerned with this Enquiry but the purchaser of industrial or warehouse premises or land will want to know of the existence of any entries, particularly if it is proposed to carry on an operation dependent upon the storage of hazardous substances (as defined). A purchaser of part, as opposed to the whole, of particular premises or land should consider applying, under s 18 of the Act, for continuation of any existing hazardous substance consent *before* completion of the purchase; failure to apply will result in automatic revocation of consent.

Enquiry 33.2(a) asks how copies of the entries may be obtained. Since the register is open to public inspection the authority should be prepared to supply copies on request, but a charge for such copies may be made.

Enquiry 33.2(b) asks where the register may be inspected. Since the administration under this Act is an extension of provisions originally contained within the Town and Country Planning Act, and in view of the similarity of the two regimes, the register is likely to be maintained within the planning department of the Council (if, as will usually be the case, the Council is the hazardous substances authority).

Appendix

The following pages contain a photoreproduction of Form CON 29

CON 29 (1991)
To be submitted in duplicate

Search No ....

ENQUIRIES OF LOCAL AUTHORITY
(1991 EDITION)

Please type or use BLOCK LETTERS

A | To

B | Property

C | Other roadways, footpaths and footways.

D | A plan in duplicate is attached — YES/NO

Optional Enquiries are to be answered (see Box G) — YES/NO

Additional enquiries are attached in duplicate on a separate sheet — YES/NO

E
Fees of £ .... are enclosed
Signed: ....
Date: ....
Reference: ....
Tel. No: ....

F | Reply to

A. Enter name and address of district or borough council for the area. If the property is near a local authority boundary, consider raising certain enquiries (e.g. road schemes) with the adjoining council.

B. Enter address and description of the property. A plan in duplicate must be attached wherever possible, and may be insisted upon by some Councils. Without a plan, replies may be inaccurate or incomplete. A plan is essential if Optional Enquiry 18 is raised.

C. Enter name and/or location (and mark on plan, if possible) any other roadways, footpaths and footways (in addition to those entered in Box B) to which enquiries 3 and (if raised) 19 are to apply.

D. Answer every question. Any additional enquiries must be attached on a separate sheet in duplicate, and an additional fee will be charged for any which the Council is willing to answer.

E. Details of fees can be obtained from the Council or from the Association of District Councils, 26 Chapter Street, London SW1P 4ND.

F. Enter name and address of person or firm lodging this form.

G. Tick the Optional Enquiries to be answered.

Please read the Notes on page 4.

G | Optional Enquiries

17 ☐	21 ☐	25 ☐	29 ☐	33 ☐
18 ☐	22 ☐	26 ☐	30 ☐	
19 ☐	23 ☐	27 ☐	31 ☐	
20 ☐	24 ☐	28 ☐	32 ☐	

PART I - STANDARD ENQUIRIES (APPLICABLE IN EVERY CASE)

DEVELOPMENT PLANS PROVISIONS
Structure Plan
1.1.1. What structure plan is in force?
1.1.2. Have any proposals been made public for the alteration of the structure plan?

Local Plans
1.2. What local plans (including action area plans) are adopted or in the course of preparation?

Old Style Development Plan
1.3. What old style development plan is in force?

Unitary Plan [1]
1.4.1. What stage has been reached in the preparation of a unitary development plan?
1.4.2. Have any proposals been made public for the alteration or replacement of a unitary development plan?

Non-Statutory Plan
1.5.1. Have the Council made public any proposals for the preparation or modification of a non-statutory plan?
1.5.2. If so, what stage has been reached?

Primary Use and Provisions for the Property
1.6. In any of the above plans or proposals:-
 (a) what primary use is indicated for the area?
 (b) what provisions are included for the property?

Land required for Public Purposes
1.7. Is the property included in any of the categories of land specified in Schedule 13 paras 5 and 6 of the T&CP Act 1990?

DRAINAGE
Foul Drainage
2.1.1. To the Council's knowledge, does foul drainage from the property drain to a public sewer [2]?
2.1.2. If so, is the connection to the public sewer effected by:
 (a) drain and private sewer, or
 (b) drain alone?

Surface Water Drainage
2.2.1. Does surface water from the property drain to a public sewer?
2.2.2. Does surface water from the property drain to a highway drain or sewer which is the subject of an agreement under s.21(1)(a) of the Public Health Act 1936?
2.2.3. If the Reply to either 2.2.1 or 2.2.2 is "Yes", is the connection to that sewer or highway drain effected by:
 (a) drain and private sewer, or
 (b) drain alone?

Combined Private Sewer
2.3. Is there in force in relation to any part of the drainage of the property an agreement under s.22 of the Building Act 1984?

Adoption Agreement
2.4.1. To the Council's knowledge, is any sewer serving, or which is proposed to serve, the property the subject of an agreement under s.18 of the Public Health Act 1936 [3]?
2.4.2. If so, is such an agreement supported by a bond or other financial security [4]?

Potential Compulsory Drainage Connection
2.5. If the Reply to either Enquiry 2.1.1 or 2.2.1 is "No", to the Council's knowledge, is there a foul or surface water sewer (as appropriate) within 100 feet of the property and at a level which makes it reasonably practicable to construct a drain from the property to that sewer? [5]

Sewerage Undertaker
2.6. Please state the name and address of the sewerage undertaker.

MAINTENANCE OF ROADS ETC
Publicly Maintained
3.1. Are all the roadways, footpaths and footways referred to in Boxes B and C on page 1 maintainable at the public expense within the meaning of the Highways Act 1980?

Resolutions to make up or adopt
3.2. If not, have the Council passed any resolution to:
 (a) make up any of those roadways, footpaths or footways at the cost of the frontagers, or
 (b) adopt any of them without cost to the frontagers?
 If so, please specify.

Adoption Agreements
3.3.1. Have the Council entered into any outstanding agreement relating to the adoption of any of those roadways, footpaths or footways? If so, please specify.
3.3.2. Is any such agreement supported by a bond or other financial security [4]?

ROAD SCHEMES
Trunk and Special Roads
4.1.1. What orders, draft orders or schemes have been notified to the Council by the appropriate Secretary of State for the construction of a new trunk or special road, the centre line of which is within 200 metres of the property?
4.1.2. What proposals have been notified to the Council by the appropriate Secretary of State for the alteration or improvement of an existing road, involving the construction, whether or not within existing highway limits, of a subway, underpass, flyover, footbridge, elevated road or dual carriageway, the centre line of which is within 200 metres of the property?

Other Roads
4.2. What proposals of their own [6] have the Council approved for any of the following, the limits of construction of which are within 200 metres of the property:-
 (a) the construction of a new road, or
 (b) the alteration or improvement of an existing road, involving the construction, whether or not within existing highway limits, of a subway, underpass, flyover, footbridge, elevated road or dual carriageway?

Road Proposals Involving Acquisition
4.3. What proposals have the Council approved, or have been notified to the Council by the appropriate Secretary of State, for highway construction or improvement that involve the acquisition of the property?

Road Proposals at Consultation Stage
4.4. What proposals have either the Secretary of State or the Council published for public consultation relating to the construction of a new road indicating a possible route the centre line of which would be likely to be within 200 metres of the property?

OUTSTANDING NOTICES
5. What outstanding statutory notices or informal notices have been issued by the Council under the Public Health Acts, Housing Acts or Highways Acts?
(This enquiry does not cover notices shown in the Official Certificate

---

[1] This enquiry relates only to London Boroughs and other metropolitan authorities.
[2] Any reply will be based on information supplied to the Council by the sewerage undertakers.
[3] The enquirer should also make similar enquiries of the sewerage undertaker, even if the Council reply to this enquiry.
[4] The enquirer should satisfy himself as to the adequacy of any bond or other financial security.
[5] If the Council cannot reply in the affirmative, the enquirer must make his own survey.
[6] This enquiry refers to the Council's own proposals and not those of other bodies or companies.

of Search or notices relating to matters covered by Enquiry 13).

BUILDING REGULATIONS
6. What proceedings have the Council authorised in respect of an infringement of the Building Regulations?

PLANNING APPLICATIONS AND PERMISSIONS
Applications and Decisions
7.1. Please list –
(a) any entries in the Register of planning applications and permissions,
(b) any applications, and decisions in respect of listed building consent and
(c) any applications, and decisions in respect of conservation area consent.

Inspection and Copies
7.2. If there are any entries:-
(a) how can copies be obtained?
(b) where can the Register be inspected?

NOTICES UNDER PLANNING ACTS
Enforcement and Stop Notices
8.1.1. Please list any entries in the Register of enforcement notices and stop notices.
8.1.2. If there are any entries:-
(a) how can copies be obtained?
(b) where can that Register be inspected?

Proposed Enforcement or Stop Notice
8.2. Except as shown in the Official Certificate of Search, or in reply to enquiry 8.1.1, has any enforcement notice, listed building enforcement notice or stop notice been authorised by the Council for issue or service (other than notices which have been withdrawn or quashed)?

Compliance with Enforcement Notices
8.3. If an enforcement notice or listed building enforcement notice has been served or issued, has it been complied with to the satisfaction of the Council?

Other Contravention Notices etc
8.4. Has the Council served, or resolved to serve, any other notice or proceedings relating to a contravention of planning control?

Listed Building Repairs Notices, etc.
8.5.1. To the knowledge of the Council, has the service of a repairs notice been authorised?
8.5.2. If the Council have authorised the making of an order for the compulsory acquisition of a listed building, is a "minimum compensation" provision included, or to be included, in the order?
8.5.3. Have the Council authorised the service of a building preservation notice? [7]

DIRECTIONS RESTRICTING PERMITTED DEVELOPMENT
9. Except as shown in the Official Certificate of Search, have the Council resolved to make a direction to restrict permitted development?

ORDERS UNDER PLANNING ACTS
Revocation Orders Etc.
10.1. Except as shown in the Official Certificate of Search, have the Council resolved to make any Orders revoking or modifying any planning permission or discontinuing an existing planning use?

Tree Preservation Order
10.2. Except as shown in the Official Certificate of Search, have the Council resolved to make any Tree Preservation Orders?

COMPENSATION FOR PLANNING DECISIONS
11. What compensation has been paid by the Council under s. 114 of the T&CP Act 1990 for planning decisions restricting development other than new development?

PRE-REGISTRATION CONSERVATION AREA
12. Except as shown in the Official Certificate of Search, is the area a conservation area?

COMPULSORY PURCHASE
13. Except as shown in the Official Certificate of Search, have the Council made any order (whether or not confirmed by the appropriate Secretary of State) or passed any resolution for compulsory acquisition which is still capable of being implemented? [8]

AREAS DESIGNATED UNDER HOUSING ACTS ETC.
Clearance
14.1. Has any programme of clearance for the area been –
(a) submitted to the Department of the Environment, or
(b) resolved to be submitted, or
(c) otherwise adopted by resolution of the Council?

Housing
14.2. Except as shown in the Official Certificate of Search, have the Council resolved to define the area as designated for a purpose under the Housing Acts? If so, please specify the purpose.

SMOKE CONTROL ORDER
15. Except as shown in the Official Certificate of Search, have the Council made a smoke control order or resolved to make or vary a smoke control order for the area?

CONTAMINATED LAND
16.1 Is the property included in the Register of contaminated land?
16.2 If so:-
(a) how can copies of the entries be obtained?
(b) where can the Register be inspected?

PART II - OPTIONAL ENQUIRIES
(APPLICABLE ONLY AS INDICATED ON PAGE ONE)

RAILWAYS
17. What proposals have been notified to the Council, and what proposals of their own have the Council approved, for the construction of a railway (including light railway or monorail) the centre line of which is within 200 metres of the property?

PUBLIC PATHS OR BYWAYS
18. Has any public path, bridleway or road used as a public path or byway which abuts on or crosses the property been shown in a definitive map or revised definitive map prepared under Part IV of the National Parks and Access to the Countryside Act 1949 or Part III of the Wildlife and Countryside Act 1981? If so, please mark its approximate route on the attached plan.

PERMANENT ROAD CLOSURE
19. What proposals have the Council approved for permanently stopping up or diverting any of the roads or footpaths referred to in Boxes B and C on page 1?

TRAFFIC SCHEMES
20. In respect of any of the roads referred to in Boxes B and C on

---

[7] The Historic Buildings and Monuments Commission also have power to issue this type of notice for buildings in London Boroughs, and separate enquiry should be made of them if appropriate.

[8] This enquiry refers to the Council's own compulsory purchase powers and not those of other bodies.

page 1, what proposals have the Council approved, but have not yet put into operation, for:-
(a) waiting restrictions,
(b) one way streets,
(c) prohibition of driving,
(d) pedestrianisation, or
(e) vehicle width or weight restrictions?

ADVERTISEMENTS
Entries in Register
21.1.1. Please list any entries in the Register of applications, directions and decisions relating to consent for the display of advertisements.
21.1.2. If there are any entries, where can that Register be inspected?

Notices, Proceedings and Orders
21.2 Except as shown in the Official Certificate of Search:
(a) has any notice been given by the Secretary of State or served in respect of a direction or proposed direction restricting deemed consent for any class of advertisement?
(b) have the Council resolved to serve a notice requiring the display of any advertisement to be discontinued?
(c) if a discontinuance notice has been served, has it been complied with to the satisfaction of the Council?
(d) have the Council resolved to serve any other notice or proceedings relating to a contravention of the control of advertisements?
(e) have the Council resolved to make an order for the special control of advertisements for the area?

COMPLETION NOTICES
22. Which of the planning permissions in force have the Council resolved to terminate by means of a completion notice under s.94 of the T&CP Act 1990?

PARKS AND COUNTRYSIDE
Areas of Outstanding Natural Beauty
23.1. Has any order under s.87 of the National Parks and Access to the Countryside Act 1949 been made?

National Parks
23.2. Is the property within a National Park designated under s.7 of the National Parks and Access to the Countryside Act 1949?

PIPE LINES
24. Has a map been deposited under s.35 of the Pipe-lines Act 1962, or Schedule 7 of the Gas Act 1986, showing a pipe-line within 100 feet of the property?

HOUSES IN MULTIPLE OCCUPATION
25. Is the property included in a registration of houses scheme (houses in multiple occupation) under s.346 of the Housing Act 1985, containing control provisions as authorised by s.347 of that Act?

NOISE ABATEMENT
Noise Abatement Zone
26.1. Have the Council made, or resolved to make, any noise abatement zone order under s.63 of the Control of Pollution Act 1974 for the area?

Entries in Register
26.2.1. Has any entry been recorded in the Noise Level Register kept pursuant to s.64 of the Control of Pollution Act 1974?
26.2.2. If there is an entry, how can copies be obtained and where can that Register be inspected?

URBAN DEVELOPMENT AREAS
27.1. Is the area an urban development area designated under Part XVI of the Local Government, Planning and Land Act 1980?
27.2 If so, please state the name of the urban development corporation and the address of its principal office.

ENTERPRISE ZONES
28. Is the area an enterprise zone designated under Part XVIII of the Local Government Planning and Land Act 1980?

INNER URBAN IMPROVEMENT AREAS
29. Have the Council resolved to define the area as an improvement area under s.4 of the Inner Urban Areas Act 1978?

SIMPLIFIED PLANNING ZONES
30.1. Is the area a simplified planning zone adopted or approved pursuant to s.83 of the T&CP Act 1990?
30.2. Have the Council approved any proposal for designating the area as a simplified planning zone?

LAND MAINTENANCE NOTICES
31. Have the Council authorised the service of a maintenance notice under s.215 of the T&CP Act 1990?

MINERAL CONSULTATION AREAS
32. Is the area a mineral consultation area notified by the county planning authority under Sched.1 para 7 of the T&CP Act 1990?

HAZARDOUS SUBSTANCE CONSENTS
33.1. Please list any entries in the Register kept pursuant to s.28 of the Planning (Hazardous Substances) Act 1990.
33.2. If there are any entries:-
(a) how can copies of the entries be obtained?
(b) where can the Register be inspected?

General Notes

(A) Unless otherwise indicated, all these enquiries relate to the property as described in Box B on page 1, and any part of that property, and "the area" means any area in which the property is located.
(B) These enquiries will not necessarily reveal (i) matters relating to properties other than the Property specified in Box B on page 1, or (ii) matters relating to land outside the area of the Council to whom these enquiries are sent, or (iii) matters which are outside the functions of that Council (although, under arrangements made between District Councils and County Councils, the replies given to certain enquiries addressed to District Councils cover knowledge and actions of both the District Council and the County Council).
(C) References to "the Council" include references to a predecessor Council and to a Committee or Sub-Committee of the Council acting under delegated powers, and to any other body or person taking action under powers delegated by the Council or a predecessor Council.
(D) References to an Act, Regulation or Order include reference to (i) any statutory provision which it replaces and (ii) any amendment or re-enactment of it.
(E) References to any Town and Country Planning Act, Order or Regulation are abbreviated, e.g. "T&CP Act 1990".
(F) The replies will be given after the appropriate enquiries and in the belief that they are in accordance with the information at present available to the officers of the replying Council(s), but on the distinct understanding that none of the Councils, nor any Council officer, is legally responsible for them, except for negligence. Any liability for negligence shall extend for the benefit of not only the person by or for whom these Enquiries are made but also a person (being a purchaser for the purposes of s.10(3) of the Local Land Charges Act 1975) who or whose agent had knowledge, before the relevant time (as defined in that section), of the replies to these Enquiries.
(G) This form of Enquiries is approved by The Law Society, the Association of County Councils, the Association of District Councils and the Association of Metropolitan Authorities and is published by their authority.

The Replies are given on the attached sheet(s)

Signed: ....
Proper Officer

Date: ....

Form Con 29 © Law Society copyright. This edition © 1991 Fourmat Publishing 133 Upper Street London N1 1QP

Index

Action areas 18
Advertisements 113–121
   definition of 114
Areas:
   action 18
   clearance 79–81
   conservation 47–49, 74–76
   housing action 82–84
   improvement, inner urban 152–154
   mineral consultation 162–164
   outstanding natural beauty, of 126–129
   renewal 83
   special control, of 120–121
   urban development 143–147
   See also *Zones*

Blight notices 19
Bridleway 99–102
   definition of 99
   stopping up or diversion of 104
Building preservation notices 60–63
Building Regulations 40–42
By-ways 99–102
   definition of 99–100

Clearance areas 79–81
Compensation for planning restriction 71–73
Completion notices 122–125
Compulsory purchase orders 35, 51, 77–78
   listed buildings, in relation to 56–60
   See also *Railways*
Consents:
   advertisements 115–116
   conservation area 47–49
   hazardous substance 165–170

177

listed building 46–47, 61
Conservation areas 47–49, 74–76
    consent, applications and decisions in relation to 47–49
Contaminated land 89–91

Development:
    completion notices, and 122–125
    enforcement notices, and 50–55
    enterprise zones, and 150
    "five year rule", and 123–124
    permitted 64–66
        restrictions on 65–66
    plans 9–19
        "old style" 13–14
    simplified planning zones, and 150
    special development orders 145
    stop notices, and 50–54
    urban development areas 143–147
    See also *Areas of outstanding natural beauty;*
        Compensation for planning restriction; National parks
Discontinuance:
    display of advertisement, of 118–119
    planning permission, of 68–69
Diversion orders 103–106
Drainage 20–26
    See also *Sewers*

Enforcement notices 50–55
Enterprise zones 148–151
Environmental Protection Act 1990 .... 89–91, 127
Experimental traffic orders 109–110
Extinguishment orders of public paths or bridleways 104

Food Safety Act 1990 37
Footpath 99–102
    definition of 28, 99
    stopping up or diversion of 104
Footway, definition of 28
Foul drainage 21–22
    potential compulsory connection of 25

Gas pipe lines 134–135
General Development Order 64–66, 75
General improvement areas 81–84
General notes 3–5

Hazardous substance consents 165–170
Health and Safety at Work Act 1974 37
Highways:
    agreements for making up 29–30
    maintenance of 27–30

Index

notices in respect of	29, 36
proposed	29–30, 31–34
stopping up or diversion of	103–106
See also *Roads*	
Housing Act 1985	36
Housing action areas	82–84
Improvement areas, inner urban	152–154
Land maintenance notices	159–161
Listed building:	
applications and decisions	48–49
building preservation notice, and	60–63
categories of	45–46
consent	46–47, 61
enforcement notice	50–55, 61
Local Land Charges, register of	1, 61, 70
Local plans	9, 12–13
primary uses, and	18
London Borough Councils, list of	39
London Building Acts	37, 38
Mineral consultation areas	162–164
Minimum compensation in relation to listed buildings,	
compulsory acquisition of	59–60
Modification of planning permissions	67–69
Multiple occupation, houses in	136–138
National parks	129–131
Noise abatement	139–142
Non-statutory plans	9, 17
blight notices, and	19
primary uses, and	18
Notices:	
advertisements, in respect of	118–120
blight	19
completion	122–125
discontinuance (of display of advertisement)	118–119
enforcement	50–55
proposed	53–54
environmental protection, in respect of	37
food safety, in respect of	37
hazardous substance contravention	169
health and safety at work, in respect of	37
highways, in respect of	29, 36
housing, in respect of	36
land maintenance	159–161
listed building enforcement	50–55, 61
proposed	53–54
noise abatement	140

pipe lines, in relation to 132–135
planning contravention 55–56
public health, in respect of 36
repairs 56–58
  compulsory purchase, and 56–60
stop 50–54
  proposed 53–54

"Old style" development plans 13–14
  primary uses, and 18
Orders:
  advertisements, in relation to control of 120–121
  areas of outstanding natural beauty, in relation to 126–129
  compulsory purchase 35, 51, 56–60, 77–78
  discontinuance, in relation to use of land 68–69
  diversion 103–106
  enterprise zone designation 149–150
  experimental traffic orders 109–110
  extinguishment 104
  modification 67–69
  national parks, in relation to 129–131
  noise abatement 139–142
  noise reduction 142
  pedestrian planning 111–112
  revocation 67–69
  rights of way, in relation to 100–102
  smoke control 85–88
  special development 145
  stopping up, in relation to roads or footpaths 103–106
  temporary traffic 110
  traffic regulation 107–109, 110
  tree preservation 69–70

Pedestrian planning orders 111–112
Pipe lines 132–135
Planning:
  applications 43–49, 50–63
    mineral consultation areas, and 162–164
  permissions 43–49, 50–63
    compensation for restriction on 71–73
    conservation areas, and 47–48, 75
    contravention notices, and 55–56
    discontinuance orders, and 68–69
    enforcement notices, and 50–55
    enterprise zones, and 150
    listed buildings, and 45–47
    revocation or modification of 67–69
    simplified planning zones, and 155–158
    stop notices, and 50–54
    termination of by completion notice 122–125
Private street works 29

Index

Public health notices 36
Public paths 99–102

Railways 95–98
  light 97–98
Register:
  advertisement consents, of 115–116
  contaminated land, of 89–91
  enforcement and stop notices, of 48, 53, 54
  hazardous substances, of 165–170
  houses in multiple occupation, of 136–138
  local land charges, of 1, 61, 70
  noise level 141–142
  planning applications, of 43–49
Renewal areas 83
Repairs notices 56–58
  compulsory purchase, and 56–60
Revocation of planning permission 67–69
Rights of way 99–102
Roads:
  constructing or altering, schemes for 31–34
    acquisition of land for 33–34
    published proposals relating to 34
  maintenance of 27–30
  special, schemes for 32–33
  stopping up or diversion of 103–106
  trunk, schemes for 32–33
Roadway, definition of 28

Sewers:
  adoption agreements relating to 24–25
  definition of 21
  private 22, 23–24
  sewerage undertakers 26
Simplified planning zones 155–158
Smoke control orders 85–88
Special control areas 120–121
Special development orders 145
Stop notices 50–54
Stopping-up orders, in relation to roads or footpaths 103–106
Structure plans 9, 10–12
  primary uses, and 18
Surface water drainage 21, 22–23
  potential compulsory connection relating to 25

Traffic schemes 107–112
Tree preservation orders 69–70

Unitary development plan 9, 11, 14–17
  primary uses, and 18
Urban:
  development areas 143–147
    special development orders, and 145

181

ENQUIRIES OF LOCAL AUTHORITIES

    development corporations 143–147
    improvement areas 152–154

Wasteland — see *Land maintenance notices*

Zones:
    enterprise 148–151
    noise abatement 139–140
    simplified planning 155–158
    See also *Areas*